Illustration by Duc duClos

Old Echoes of a New Voice

Duc du Clos

Copyright © 2009 Duc du Clos

All rights reserved. No part of this publication may be reproduced, stored in a retrieval system, or transmitted, in any form or by any means, electronic, mechanical, photocopying, recording, or otherwise, without the written permission of the author.

A catalogue record of this book is available from
The American Library of Congress
2009904500

ISBN 978-0-615-28891-8

Cover: Planetware

Punctuation has been inserted in adages, proverbs, quotes and poems to create a pause, and therefore may not always follow literary rules.

Books may be purchased @ **Quotediem.com** among other sites
Soon available in **French**, **Spanish** and **Italian**

Printed by:
Sterling Pierce
395 Atlantic Avenue
East Rockaway, NY 11518

Dedications

... **To my sons, Jhan-Duc, Gian, Chrizian and Mekael:** my four cardinal points, without whom, I would be lost. I love you.

... **To my wife:** the center of my life, from whom those points evolve. Your love will forever and eternally be my last breath.

... **To my loving mother, Julia, brothers Patrick and Massaryck, and sisters Carine and Dayana:** whose rays of sun warm my heart. I am proud to be one of you.

... **To the spirit of my dear father**, the constant light of my inspiration. I so miss your love and affection.

... **To my grandmother Juliannie**, who nurtured my heart and soul 'till her last days. May your spirit be preserved.

... **To my family & relatives:** who have stood and are still standing by me. You are my found treasure.

... **To Jean Claude Armand and family:** a blessing to this earth.

... **To Count Louis de Maigret, Baron de Stockem and family:** May you inspire the minds in heaven as you did mine here. Thank-you for having taken the time to show me its importance.

...**To my friends and laureate colleagues:** Thank you for your kind support. Your roots are the strength I continue to rely upon.

...**To Marie-Rose Wagnac:** Thank-you for everything.

... **To the old century poets:** who have inspired me since my early years; help me do the same for others, so our world will live on.

... **And finally, to my readers:** Thank-you! And may this book be a source of enjoyment among friends and family, as you become an extension of me... the new branches of my poetree.

Duc

Contents

Editor's Preface	iv
Faded Memory	v
Author's Thoughts	vi
Authors Definitions	vii

Adages, Proverbs, Quotes:

… Romantic	1
… Athleticism	35
… Educational	47
… Inspirational	65
… Heroism	291
… Faith	301
… Friendship	311

Poetry: 321

The Silhouette	322
The Painted Mind	324
I Matter	326
Dix Honest Hombres	327
Heroes	328
The Difference	330
Angel	331
The Same Theory	332
My Existence	333

Contents *(cont)*

Joy & Happiness	334
A World Revealed	335
Our Planet	336
"I", Who Am Part of "If"	338
Love is Like the Sea	339
True Friends	340
Whole	342
The Art of Science	344
A Good Friend	346
The Romantic	347
A Shade Apart	348
The Demon Within	350
The Prose and Cons of a Poem	351
The Punctuation Points ...	352
My Child	353
Me	354
My Prayer	356
You, Once Again	358
The Dove of Rome	360
Time	362
Night	364
The Mind Is Like A Shelf	365
Dad	366

Editor's Preface

This New Era

As we approach this new era... as the rainbow adorns a new shade on its prism, and as the bells of time ring a new tone, a young nation embraces a new challenge. It is indeed an accomplishment of magnitude and historic value. Yet, if it's simply perceived as a victory, the battle is then just beginning.

We will have to keep in mind that a single string does not braid. It is only by intertwining can we collectively find the strength to weave the rope, which will pull us to safety. We shall cease to falter on neglect, for oversight is a state too often bypassed on the way to blinded success.

Today in the making of history, I woke up a man of irreplaceable complexion, a shade of incandescent distinction. I find myself strutting with a different cadence, as if with each step, the ground beneath my weight holds stronger, inviting the next step to be taken with greater assurance. The same old air feels crisper than usual, not that the world has changed, rather that we as humans, finally caught up to a page in the book of old... that we are all created, not necessarily equal, but most importantly, at the image of a greater figure.

We may here, on earth, rejoice in exultation. But the smile that I'm sure we have painted on the face of our creator is one of pure and eternal pride. He knew that it was going to take us some enduring time, but he also knew we could, and would; for the testaments are not wasted scriptures. And if we fulfill his requests, even one per lifetime, we may still have a chance at redemption.

Our souls have reached a new flight. However, as we ascend to higher destination, the clouds shall challenge but not impede our visions. We can't afford to look back at the past and its tumultuous grievances, nor down at the present and its fear of failure. Our sight and objective should remain steadfast. To a future of unparalleled endeavors, we shall test our strengths.

With compassionate hands we will shake those in need. Our neighbors may be far, but in our hearts, they are just a thought away, for this era is one for human kind.

Dedicated to **The United Nations**   *Duc du Clos*

Faded Memories

Remembering when I was young, I was often told that I was gifted with words. My answer was always that with such a gift, I would only be exposing the vulnerability of my heart. I would have then traded it for a more tangible present, something more concrete, which could be felt and protected in the palm of my hands. I never realized that the strength of sincere sentiments was much greater than that of physical hands.

In those early days of my life, I was viewed as an old soul, like the poets of old centuries who often lived on the verge of insanity. I was then sixteen and most of my writing was primarily in French, with some in Spanish. In my youthfulness, I was unaware that my poems would ever become something I would cherish. So regrettably, I gave them all away. My focus turned to singing, painting and athletics. All the while, I felt that my emotions were still bursting in my heart. It wasn't until I was in my twenties when I, once again, felt the urge to recapture the many sentiments, which were still slowly running through my veins.

Today, as maturity teaches me the value of old poetry still echoing in my heart, I found a new voice. In that spirit, I would like to share with you my most intimate and deepest emotions. As you travel through these pages, may my thoughts come alive in your hands, for it is my gift of words to you.

... Enjoy!

My dream is not to have the whole world know me, for that can change me for the worse. It is to know the world in which I live, so I can change it for the better.

Our legacy, if only by the concrete or metal wings we leave behind, will never help our soul take flight.

Duc du Clos

Author's Thoughts

The real truth *is not on the lips of many, but rather in the hearts of a few.*

The effort spent on blame *is so much more productive in the search and application of remedial solutions.*

Without its "li", *"religion" could never condemn another by the **"region"** it was borne.*

It is difficult to ink *for the simple mind. The least they get me, the more I appreciate the few who can and do.*

One will always hear *much more than it actually is and will eventually know so much less.*

Duc du Clos

Author's Definitions

A quote *is a framed statement, while an adage is a statement, which can be quoted to frame an appropriate moment.*

An adage *... simply needs to be ordinarily misunderstood to be appreciated. Once fully comprehended, it becomes extraordinary.*

A proverb *... is an expression, which might wisely add age to your wisdom.*

A quote *... is an art, which allows, invites, and forgives individual misinterpretations.*

Duc du Clos

Adages

Proverbs

Quotes

Whoever said *not to judge a book by its cover was not its author,
for the cover is the first impression of its content.*
Duc du Clos

Adages, Proverbs & Quotes:

Romantic

Loving is *the first obligation of the heart, then comes its beating.*

Duc du Clos

Sex is *as cool as ice sculptures. Once melted, its liquid volume can never depict its statuesque beauty, but as a slippery surface.*

Duc du Clos

It does not matter *your destination, if you don't let love guide you… you will never get there.*

Duc du Clos

Before you offer *the world to someone, first take inventory of what is yours. It is of such personal possession that the gift will be valued and appreciated.*

Duc du Clos

Once born, *real love never truly dies. It only gets covered by other emotions, to which we pay more attention, or endorse stronger values… until a mere shadow from the old past strikes its resurrection.*

Duc du Clos

Illusion *is your worst enemy, while imagination is your best weapon.*

Duc du Clos

The frame *that's one's heart is always ready to endorse the painting of another's love.*

Duc du Clos

There's often...
    ... *a crash after a crush.*

Duc du Clos

The difference between having sex and making love is that by making love, one increases an area of emotion; and by simply having sex, although one releases tension from such action, one is also left with less emotion.

Duc du Clos

When you are the train of thoughts, which constantly glides on the tracks of someone else's mind, an immense pleasure and contentment is discovered at every stop.

Duc du Clos

Just the flicker radiating from a special glance can sometime easily enflame the most protected soul.

Duc du Clos

In love, *if there was ever enough room to fall, there will always be plenty to stand and make it work.*

Duc du Clos

A heart *is rather too big of a home for one alone to live in.*

Duc du Clos

A heart *is like an evergreen. A bird upon its peak, serenading its branches, will keep it warm and never would it lose its leaves, even in winter.*

Duc du Clos

In love, *as it is in nature, a seed which was yesterday planted, even today grown big as a tree, still needs yesterday's sweet care.*

Duc du Clos

Sex *is like homework, which can be performed anywhere, even in a school bus; but on exam day, it is held in the heart, a class of its own.*

Duc du Clos

If one rewinds *yesterday's memory, perhaps they'll pinpoint where the picture has blemished.*

Duc du Clos

Before *you trust in love, believe in the agony of its pains.*

Duc du Clos

Some people *are so short of self-esteem that it's in stepping on someone else's shoe they can see over the fence of their own life.*

Duc du Clos

Relationships *are like the Sunday paper. The moment you pull it out of its crisp structure and read it, it is almost impossible to put it back to its original appeal.*

Duc du Clos

Sometimes love is such a fragile feeling that it should only be handled by the hands of a heart.

Duc du Clos

Love is not a tree for adults to damage or cut down, but a foundation upon which birds can build their nest to love and multiply.

Duc du Clos

The language of passion is made of light expressions and tender moments of pleasure.

Duc du Clos

Love *is part of two halves of time. The first half is to be anxious and scared, and the other half to reminisce and laugh about the first half.*

Duc du Clos

A true love *is sometimes like a dusty piece of furniture covered by years of disregard. Yet, it still remains beautiful, if only one would take the time to sweep away the faded hours.*

Duc du Clos

Love gets lovelier *as it leaves on its journey for greater destination.*

Duc du Clos

My mind *works only when I think of you and aches when I don't think of you. So needless to say, it does not pay not to think of you.*

Duc du Clos

If there's one thing *I don't miss, it's missing you, because I still do... oh so much.*

Duc du Clos

Always try to renew your love as often as possible, as it is like a flower, and time can't wait to wither its petals.

Duc du Clos

When love becomes an ache, it should be confined to your heart and not go to your head.

Duc du Clos

Sometimes the most magnificent picture can haunt the mind, like the tides of the sea ... most unpreventable, and always unpredictable, as they brush the shore of your thoughts.

Duc du Clos

One may be a fool in love, but one should be a genius in loving one another.

Duc du Clos

The wonder of the heart often brings pain to the thought of loving.

Duc du Clos

If one pervades one's soul with joy and happiness, there'll be very little room in the heart for sadness.

Duc du Clos

A broken heart is, at the very least, a sign of an existential one.

Duc du Clos

The tears we don't shed are the ones filling up the pool of our hearts, in which we so often drown.

Duc du Clos

To illuminate *and find their way back home, the evening stars often borrow the rays from your eyes.*

Duc du Clos

Love *is the only gift, which is born wrapped by the natural tissue of the heart.*

Duc du Clos

It is *rather difficult to be certain that anyone is the love of someone else's life. Yet, it is practical for someone to be the life of another's love, for one's presence may keep it nourished and alive.*

Duc du Clos

We should all *take a chance on love, for it is much more consoling to have your heart broken from falling, than having it intact, living and standing alone.*

Duc du Clos

Some people *believe that love is a rose, which might explain the fading and loss of its petals the moment it opens up to the wrong temperature.*

Duc du Clos

Love *means to always be next in particular, and consideration is to always be parallel in general.*

Duc du Clos

Despite *our accomplishment, until we live for another's heart, we have yet to live.*

Duc du Clos

Love necessitates passion… *the embrace of another searching soul.*

Duc du Clos

Happiness in life *is like coins in a piggy bank; they should be disbursed and enjoyed with the same patience of insertion, one coin at a time. Otherwise, you'll just break the bank that's your heart.*

Duc du Clos

When you fall *in love for the first time, however hard it may be, expect to make a fool's recovery, for you will do it again.*

Duc du Clos

Forgiveness *is opening an inviting door, allowing the pain, which came through yesterday's window, greater passage to escape.*

Duc du Clos

Forget the heart! *True love elevates your soul and sends it afloat above all spirits.*

Duc du Clos

An adage... *is like a symphony. It is heard and read with the heart in silence. If you can't feel the music with your eyes closed, then you might as well cover your ears.*

Duc du Clos

If you admire and respect the rose and only want a petal, you'll be spared its thorns, for there won't be a need to grab its stem.

Duc du Clos

Be a whole lot happier...

... care a little.

Duc du Clos

Love is giving up one's part, which makes another whole.

Duc du Clos

A heart *is like a beautiful sunflower. Within its center, it evenly supports all feelings and emotions, though seemingly separated, yet connected petals.*

Duc du Clos

If you think *you can touch the part, which can change a human, you'll be disappointed, for it's not the heart.*

Duc du Clos

Even when love does not work out, still, it is never less than love. It is just a different kind of love.

Duc du Clos

If I ever have to lose you, I pray it be to myself.

Duc du Clos

In any relationship, compatibility is learned through sacrifices.

Duc du Clos

True happiness *is not programmable, dependable, nor reliable. It is a formula with such ever-changing ingredients that it can only be natural.*

Duc du Clos

Affection *is the sincere expression of care, concern, and love, without any other obvious reasons.*

Duc du Clos

Love may be a hurting thing, but there's not another thing like love.

Duc du Clos

One who has been gifted by the love of others, should only live for the opportunity of reciprocity.

Duc du Clos

The burden of love is often on the heart to show evidentiary proof of sincerity.

Duc du Clos

The fear *of love only deepens its need.*

Duc du Clos

Love *is the ultimate cliff of sacrifice; don't stand at its edge if you are scared of the risk to fall.*

Duc du Clos

***The heart,** which loves blindly, may be a fool. But the fool who loves with reservations, will never, with full extent, experience the joy of seeing with just the heart.*

Duc du Clos

***In time** of overwhelming confusion, the heart is your best compass.*

Duc du Clos

***Jealousy** is the hunchback sibling of appreciation.*

Duc du Clos

Only a heart *made of stone can become brittle enough to be permanently broken. Otherwise, its tender nature will leave it flexible to love again.*

Duc du Clos

If you admire and appreciate someone for whom you feel they are, congratulations! However, if you like someone for what they say they are, just beware.

Duc du Clos

It may be neither the right turn, nor the right time, but love is always a turn on the road, no matter when you take it, and will naturally take its turn on you.

Duc du Clos

In any relationship or encounter, one is initially granted admiration, appreciation and value… and in time, you as well, will be taken for granted.

Duc du Clos

A great relationship *is more than an alliance. It is the comfort you find in someone else other than in yourself… and as reliance, one on whom you rely to come through in time of need, such as your right hand, which holds the fingers on which you can count.*

Duc du Clos

The success *of a happy marriage is keeping her happier day by day, while desperately looking for ways to make her happiest.*

Duc du Clos

When you *are loved, it often goes to your head. But when you love, it simply comes out of your heart.*

Duc du Clos

Reliance breathes through trust*, and trust is the bedrock of calming comfort.*

Duc du Clos

Learned love *is developed like a comfort…*

Habitually,
  Physiologically,
    Psychologically,
      Dependably,
        … Finally comfortably.

Duc du Clos

Passion *is not a value, rather a virtue, which can't be taught nor passed on.*

Duc du Clos

No feeling *nor emotion retains its original and initial weight. It eventually increases or decreases.*

Duc du Clos

Your state of mind, *once known to some friends, will become a stage to perform the comedy of your life at your own expense.*

Duc du Clos

The heart *is like a cascade; it may not hold its resource for long, but it is always flowing and offers at the very least, a beauty to the senses to behold.*

Duc du Clos

Relationships *are like your favorite drinks on the rocks; if you don't enjoy them on time, they will simply and eventually be in deep water.*

Duc du Clos

Adages, Proverbs

&

Quotes:

Athletic

I perfectly possess *twice as many flaws as I do talent, and God knows I have talent.*

Duc du Clos

The person *whom you are was created by an infallible force of nature. From it the person you've become is forged by life's circumstances.*

Duc du Clos

Justification *is a well-balanced scale. You can't give an excuse of being right without giving a reason why someone else is wrong.*

Duc du Clos

There exists
      3 Kinds of Players…

      *… **A gifted** player works hard and well, even at the bottom level.*

      *… **A talented** player improves his game every day at others' level.*

      *… **An intelligent** player improvises at any situation above all levels.*

Duc du Clos

Before you get fixed on your game, fix your play.

Duc du Clos

Soccer, basketball, and other *team activities are simple sports with intricate thinking to simplify one's game.*

Duc du Clos

Because we are humans, *we're bound to err, although it was never our planned destination.*

Duc du Clos

In sports, *confidence is like water in the body or surrounding the globe. It is greater than we are, we can emerge and use it to our advantage, or it can overcome us as we drown within ourselves.*

Duc du Clos

Juggling *is about anatomical memorization, while playing the actual game is about intellectual and adjustable improvisation.*

Duc du Clos

Fatigue *is the hidden obstacle of all obvious poor performances.*

Duc du Clos

Mental fatigue *impedes your physical performance, while physical fatigue frustrates your mental performance.*

Duc du Clos

Professional Parents*, who guide their children well, eventually become parents of professionals.*

Duc du Clos

An individual mistake *is often a collective loss. However, a winning team is always an individual success.*

Duc du Clos

In a world of *runner-ups, to acquire a total and perfect winning attitude, one needs a magnitude of exactitude.*

Duc du Clos

Being second is a most perfect starting point to becoming first.

Duc du Clos

We all believe in something, not believing in anything is a belief in itself.

Duc du Clos

Visible muscles are those, which are not smart enough to conceal their strength, as does the mind.

Duc du Clos

A great leader has to, once in a while, become a decent misleader, at the very price of his good conscience.

Duc du Clos

Play every minute as if it was the last, for it is at the last minute one loses the game. If it never comes, you will never lose.

Duc du Clos

Nothing is worth the competition where the prize is greater than the competitor.

Duc du Clos

Playing *any competitive sport is a challenge within itself, and playing a step above one's expected level is an exceptional threshold.*

Duc du Clos

Victory *over an unprovoked and incomparable opponent is simply tyranny.*

Duc du Clos

Knowing your body well *enough is your best instrument in playing any sport.*

Duc du Clos

If you want to breathe easier in the game, sweat much harder at practice.

Duc du Clos

Exaggerate your practice to simplify your game.

Duc du Clos

If winning is everything, it is thus implied that losing is nothing. So why fight so desperately against nothing.

Duc du Clos

When you think *you're good, rethink your game and make it exceptional.*

Duc du Clos

Losing *is a lesson never taught, thus, never learned. But we are always tested on it. It's no wonder we always fail at it.*

Duc du Clos

Winning is for losers *when the play is not fair.*

Duc du Clos

Adages, Proverbs & Quotes:

Educational

It is very hard to teach well without explaining, and even harder to learn without comprehensive explanations.

Duc du Clos

A mind unexposed to learning is a bolder, which will never feel the creative chisels of a sculptor.

Duc du Clos

Some people *believe education is a level one reaches to be respected by others; when in fact, it is the standard which teaches one how to respect others.*

Duc du Clos

Kids *should measure their words twice before allowing their tongue to cut their words, even once.*

Duc du Clos

Beware *of any "I" trying to proceed "were", forcing "was" out such sentence. For it does not make any sense to use or abuse "were" at any location where "I" is present with any tense, which is deservingly and longingly overdue to "was". (i.e. "If I were you", for the condition doesn't change the tense).*

Duc du Clos

A mind, *which does not read, will miss the turning page in the book of success.*

Duc du Clos

The fear *and hesitation of helping others will never be greater than the satisfaction of doing so.*

Duc du Clos

Plan ahead. *If you are not certain where the next step will be, you can't plant the present one with full assurance.*

Duc du Clos

Academics *are a medium to simply help you scratch the surface of your mind, while hoping the sensation of the itch remains and lingers in said mind forever.*

Duc du Clos

Experience *will often get you through your daily routine, however, only intelligence will help you succeed in extraordinary situations.*

Duc du Clos

Behaviors *depict personal evaluations and impressions, while possessions reflect social misconceptions.*

Duc du Clos

Our personal ignorance *is the voice, which often carves and proclaims other's ingenuity.*

Duc du Clos

Teaching is having *the knowledge of passing it on.*

Duc du Clos

Our legacy *should not be made of stone, to simply build an edifice, rather stones to form a path for innocent minds to shape the principles of our visions.*

Duc du Clos

Bullies *are like simple waves. No matter how high and strong they get, in time, they always become flat as ripples on the sea.*

Duc du Clos

Teaching *well is the art of knowing how to clearly and simply reiterate that learning is endless.*

Duc du Clos

Philosophy… *is the study of the eighth sea, for it takes you to the deepest layer of the mind.*

Duc du Clos

Education *and inspiration are like breezes on a hot day. You can't have too many open doors.*

Duc du Clos

Teaching should be more than a mere transfer of information; it should be the carving of an immortalized section of the mind.

Duc du Clos

Teaching is a descriptive process, which tends to stop at understanding; while learning is a constant and absorbing affect, permeating the mind through every open and willing pore.

Duc du Clos

A bully *is the single, off-key voice in the choir, not by search of harmony, but by sheer ignorance, a note out of pitch.*

Duc du Clos

Books *are the stones of the mind. They can be used to build or destroy.*

Duc du Clos

A bully *is a small picture in a big frame, who often tries to fill up the borders by his misbehaviors.*

Duc du Clos

They say...

"Life is Academic"

... *History* will always repeat itself

... *Science* is a proven fact

... *Math* can be a never-ending equation

... *Social Studies* is an ever evolving discovery, and

... *Physics*, well, is just about matter, which matters.

Duc du Clos

An educated mind, *which is treated well, unlike an empty fountain, never runs dry, for it is a constant source of knowledge.*

Duc du Clos

Bullies *are like explosives; it is in reducing mountains into pebbles, can the vision of their muse fit in their mind.*

Duc du Clos

There's no better key *than education for life's in and outs, while ignorance is a constant lock in motion of ups and downs.*

Duc du Clos

Mistakes should be incidental, not the result of incompetency.

Duc du Clos

There exists too many people with too many thoughts about one, for one to worry about their validity in one's single mind.

Duc du Clos

Not learning anything new today is escaping a great future, while skipping a very good present.

Duc du Clos

Luck *is fickle and temporary.   Comprehension is permanent.*

Duc du Clos

The joy of a great mind *is the intelligent journey of daily learning.*

Duc du Clos

Setting an artful mind *afloat to freedom is restricting ignorance from running dumb and free.*

Duc du Clos

Scandals *are the late ceremony joyously celebrated by those who were not initially invited.*

Duc du Clos

Our expectation *is what limits and impedes us from teaching well. If one is already expected to understand, explanation is then carelessly vague, and lacks fulfillment.*

Duc du Clos

The guide, *at a certain point of the expedition, often becomes chief, for only he knows the path and its perils.*

Duc du Clos

***Between us**,* everyday one has to make a difference by teaching that there exists no difference.

Duc du Clos

What has already happened in life can never be undone. Its lesson is to mitigate its effect and prevent its reoccurrence.

Duc du Clos

We can't help having a fraction of fear, but we can overcome our fear of fractions.

Duc du Clos

Someone's past achievements *can't guarantee another's future success. It is much wiser to evaluate how well the two can share their common present.*

Duc du Clos

Adages, Proverbs & Quotes:

Inspirational

My dream is not to have the whole world know me, for that can change me for the worst. It is however, to know the world in which I live, so I can change it for the better.

Duc du Clos

This magnificent world would lose its luster without its "L" and would be a different word.

Duc du Clos

A book of poetry is like a glass of water. Every house needs one and one day it will be your turn to sip.

Duc du Clos

Landing on the right leaf, *a single drop of rain will certainly make its way down and feed its roots.*

Duc du Clos

Poets have two choices: *speak their mind at the risk of having their heart broken or speak their heart at the risk of losing their mind.*

Duc du Clos

Life's a joke, *which should be taken seriously with a smile on one's face.*

Duc du Clos

A good attitude is a well-distinguished, yet imaginative high; applied visibly accurate, it will surely exceed your actual size.

Duc du Clos

To acquire and proclaim a language, which is not of native, is to acclaim its confusion with your own, by a certain degree.

Duc du Clos

Your true and real value is far to be the one you give to yourself, but one given to you by others.

Duc du Clos

The world and kindness *are both free. Even when the world does not offer you kindness, kindness will always offer you the world.*

Duc du Clos

We all *are like bulbs in the dark. Until we are lit, we are useless, as no color is bright enough. For only clear has no doubt, shade, nor dye. It is not the complexion one has, but which reflection and value one brings to this dark world.*

Duc du Clos

Giving *has very little value if the receiving has no appreciation.*

Duc du Clos

In revenge *of your own past poverty or misfortune, help someone else reach their vengeance a bit sooner over their present tribulations.*

Duc du Clos

In terms of giving, *a taker rarely uses the same skills or scales.*

Duc du Clos

If the child in you has to die in order for you to become a grown up, the elderly in you needs not to come out, knowing that this present time will also have, by dying, wasted its turn.

Duc du Clos

Being a sensible person does not determine your range of sensibility towards others. For at times, it is not necessarily how you feel, rather, how you make someone else feel in spite of yourself.

Duc du Clos

Live much higher than simply surviving, and when you come to just survive, it will be much easier.

Duc du Clos

It's only a lie that needs the crutches of an alibi. The truth is always strong enough to stand alone.

Duc du Clos

Receiving has no joy, if the giving is not thoughtfully and sincerely shared.

Duc du Clos

The most beautiful *plants to your eyes should be those grown from the seeds once planted by your own hands.*

Duc du Clos

When two or more *people of common ground, race or religion speak of another person, thoughtfulness is very far to be what they have in common… or that certain third party would have been involved in that conversation.*

Duc du Clos

Racism *is like a broken toy. Until you take the time to understand and appreciate the difference and the many aspects of its mechanism, you cannot fix it. Meanwhile, others are happily playing with theirs, while yours remains in dire needs of repair.*

Duc du Clos

***If one works** hard enough to sweep away the bad, one will find a corner clean enough to store the good.*

Duc du Clos

***The simplicity of minds** can never level the grandiosity of thoughts.*

Duc du Clos

***Dream** is the air we breathe, reality the smell of its presence. So let's breathe in the improbable dreams.*

Duc du Clos

It's very, very wonderful to be a beautiful person, but it's even much more beautiful to be even just a mere wonderful person.

Duc du Clos

The difference between a mate and a divorcee is that the divorcee exploits to explore, while the mate may explore to simply exploit.

Duc du Clos

To be free, *one would work to the edge of insanity, and to be insane without being free is to become unfairly crazy.*

Duc du Clos

The sweet result *of any successful art is always preceded by the agony of its inspiration.*

Duc du Clos

The true story *about a lie is still a true story.*

Duc du Clos

When you're tired dealing with others, start with your conscience and it will fairly judge the situation with an impartial ruling.

Duc du Clos

A good attitude heightens your altitude, and an extended determination always carries on to realization.

Duc du Clos

Some couples share *one's life together today,*
and save an individual one to live alone tomorrow.

Duc du Clos

Some happiness *tastes as bad as sadness*
when you don't know the difference.

Duc du Clos

The thought or intent *to succeed is the first*
fitting of a king's crown by an upcoming royal jeweler.

Duc du Clos

The forgotten rays *of sun one once witnessed, always mean hope, it's beginning or ending, depending on what glare follows.*

Duc du Clos

A true business mind *never trades titles by promotion to the corporate ladder. It only adds, not knowing when it might slip off, and need the lower step.*

Duc du Clos

No tears *are hotter than the ones you shed when you are sad and feel cold inside.*

Duc du Clos

Be human! *Never make enemies on this earth. As you walk it… make amends every step of the way.*

Duc du Clos

Courage *is a beast needing to be constantly fed, even in time of diminished provision.*

Duc du Clos

Death is a long way to go. However, so lazy we are, we sometimes, unknowingly choose the short way to its destination.

Duc du Clos

Even when standing still, one has to learn to move deeply within oneself, as fast as if to avoid lightning and others' flaring perceptions.

Duc du Clos

There isn't a *better time to cry than when you're doing so, otherwise you would do it every, and all day.*

Duc du Clos

Making new friends *is likely the building a future enemy.*

Duc du Clos

I so often *have writers block, that had I kept them all, I could have built The Great Wall of China.*

Duc du Clos

When one *skips maturity, it's like wearing the cap of youth forever, while the body disintegrates.*

Duc du Clos

Forgive the ignorant, *for he's only the fruit, and allow not the innocent mind to take shade under its tree.*

Duc du Clos

The fruit of ignorance *never falls far from the tree of the unknown.*

Duc du Clos

If you think and behave *like the Norm, you'll be wasting your life on a barstool.*

Duc du Clos

The virtue of a child *is innocence, while the maturity of an adult is experience.*

Duc du Clos

When a joke *is not funny, the comedian may be forgiven for a bad sense of delivery. But on the other hand, the recipient may be lacking a more important sense, which we, who have it, call humor.*

Duc du Clos

Impression *is like a raging fire burning your sight at first glance. It's only in time you will notice an array of different shades glowing a spectacle of admiration.*

Duc du Clos

Fame *is like a ladder. As it takes you higher, be aware and count the steps, for ultimately, it has a last one.*

Duc du Clos

What *you do often enough will eventually become something you do well, yet what well you do, if rarely done, will amount to mediocrity.*

Duc du Clos

A habit *is a preprogrammed mentality, which comes on automatically at the click of a thought.*

Duc du Clos

If you have to ask or demand respect, it is not worth receiving.

Duc du Clos

To think *is to allow your brain the freedom to consciously take over the realm of possibilities.*

Duc du Clos

We often accuse *the world of the sins of our own thoughts out of fear that our minds won't withstand the burden of their sentences.*

Duc du Clos

If you can't find satisfaction and pleasure in the simple things in life, when they come on greater occasions, the joy will not long last.

Duc du Clos

Doing wrong can be done at a commonly idiotic glance. It is doing right, which requires an exceptional keen sense of intelligent contemplation.

Duc du Clos

In search *of the ultimate crown keep in mind: the more unique its jewels, the more envy it invites.*

Duc du Clos

Pressure *is an emotional condition, which presses us to rush to irrational and unplanned actions.*

Duc du Clos

The answer *to a habitual problem is not necessarily its solution, if a lesson is not learned in preventing its reoccurrence.*

Duc du Clos

***We may possess** the world and all its gold, but we will only own the person whom we are, for being is the only and ultimate possession of all.*

Duc du Clos

***Everything** costs something, regardless of how free it is.*

Duc du Clos

***Fear** is the sensation the inside feels, not knowing and wondering if the outside can actually see what goes on inside.*

Duc du Clos

If your extravagant funeral is the object replacing the sadness in hearts of loved ones, riches might have been all you left behind.

Duc du Clos

A past favor, which is mentioned or brought up in the present, is often subject to future refusal.

Duc du Clos

It is not enough to have children with patience, but to also have patience with children.

Duc du Clos

Fear is the incapacity of assessment.

Duc du Clos

In life, always be cautious. Take the unnecessary measures seriously.

Duc du Clos

Fear of falling may be great, but it should rather be viewed, at the very least, as an accomplishment of having once achieved greater heights.

Duc du Clos

Suspicion *is a disgruntled guide; not only does it lead you on the wrong path, it tends to make you take note and read into anything.*

Duc du Clos

A title *is a protective helmet for the sensitive mind against greater elements of society.*

Duc du Clos

If the farm *is sold, it is needless to keep the manure and its fragrance.*

Duc du Clos

Eggnorance *is a raw situation which will perpetually leave us scrambling through life.*

Duc du Clos

When you are *among others, and are the only one to see the* IMAGE, *the word may be missing an* "R" *for* MIRAGE.

Duc du Clos

The moment *that what you do is all that matters, you are personally yet to.*

Duc du Clos

The sin of a father, *which is inherited by a son, is the injustice on another soul.*

Duc du Clos

Don't judge me *by what eyes see, rather by what I say.*

Duc du Clos

We have to *invest and take stock in our present family before they become our future relatives.*

Duc du Clos

If your adventure *is led or simply guided, it will be a challenge to return to your point of departure from your destination… It is only from your own understanding can you retrace your path.*

Duc du Clos

When you have *the power in any situation, you feel strong and alive, because power is a living feeling. But remember, as it is borne, it is bound to not just diminish, but eventually also die.*

Duc du Clos

It is best to have 40% of security and reliance than wobble and glide over 60% of indecisive, doubtful suspicion.

Duc du Clos

Regrets are yesterday's clouds obstructing today's horizon for tomorrow's clarity.

Duc du Clos

Aspiration without inspiration is but a dream.

Duc du Clos

Life is an investment, *daily living is a transaction. It pays dividends when you're kind, and accrues remorseful penalties when you're not.*

Duc du Clos

Financially, *those without the means are endlessly limited, and those with, are perpetually and increasingly seeking for more.*

Duc du Clos

In the beginning, *it is a bit odd to think that every little bit adds up at the end.*

Duc du Clos

Across the sea, *the shores are always made of gold.*

Duc du Clos

What you did yesterday *may be gone by today. However, what you're learning today, will still have been learned by tomorrow.*

Duc du Clos

Bottles & cans ... *may be useless empty, but all can be useful in saving this planet*

Duc du Clos

Angels gently fly, *spirits swiftly flow, while power on earth is weighed per pound. So count how much you exude, and exercise it well, for it will be a load on the flight to heaven.*

Duc du Clos

The truth *can always be said and left behind you. Only a lie has the wings to catch up with you.*

Duc du Clos

One can matter *knowing one can matters.*

Duc du Clos

Discouragement *comes only from within and especially by lack of self-satisfaction.*

Duc du Clos

When only *the bottom line matters, make sure it is not far a distance when you fall, for you might not find any friendly cushions in-between.*

Duc du Clos

Whoever makes *an emotional decision and believes it's final, just begins to think about it.*

Duc du Clos

The Future *is to dream about, the Present to show off about, the Past to brag about.*

Duc du Clos

With time *value decreases, yet along grows appreciation.*

Duc du Clos

A chance *is the imperfection of 100 percent.*

Duc du Clos

Whatever talent or beauty we think we possess in our mind, in someone else's eyes, the opinion is always at a debate.

Duc du Clos

You can't always worry about what you have to lose; after all, we only suffer the consequences in what we choose.

Duc du Clos

***If you can** only read between the lines, don't count on your peripheral vision.*

Duc du Clos

***Perception** is another's unspoken explanation.*

Duc du Clos

***Between living well** and a life well lived, I'll choose the later, for a well can always run dry.*

Duc du Clos

The only thing that's worse than judging the people you meet by the people you've met, is judging the people you'll meet by the people you've heard of.

Duc du Clos

Each track has it's own path. If they lead you to the same destination, it was then only a big hole in the center of a common ground.

Duc du Clos

Existence *is like a fork, though living may cut like a knife. You eventually have to choose which way you want to live.*

Duc du Clos

Remember in life, *even a weak leaf can be a heavy burden, if you don't move on.*

Duc du Clos

Today, *don't just learn to avoid yesterday's mistakes, correct them so tomorrow can be free of them.*

Duc du Clos

At times, *it's easier to forget the price of a beautiful experience that one once enjoyed, than the reminding cost of a painful situation, like the price of marriage and the cost of divorce.*

Duc du Clos

Everyone makes infernal mistakes, which they hope will turn into ashes. Only the exceptional few can rise above the smoke to apologize.

Duc du Clos

The falling leaf which grazes your shoulder, can only be a slippery disaster to your follower, unless you're standing still, waiting for the next season.

Duc du Clos

***Admission** is a true coat of primer over an unfortunate lie to be painted by an honest apology.*

Duc du Clos

***Life** is like a cup of foaming espresso; it is never really fully filled to the rim.*

Duc du Clos

***I have one word** for the people who love me, and two for those who don't. The one word is love.*

Duc du Clos

Doubt is what makes us certain that we don't know for sure.

Duc du Clos

If one does not consider oneself as being immune to the glance of guilt, one can never assess nor understand the blaze of another's guilt.

Duc du Clos

Whatever it is, whatever it will be, one should only have half of a lot.

Duc du Clos

The thickness, consistency, and purity of red and white cells in the blood, can always, when necessary, connect to bridge the distance separating two members of the same family.

Duc du Clos

Pride is like a flame, which bursts once, keeping you warm for a single moment, then leaves you to be forgotten. Shame is the ash it leaves behind, which will stay with you as reminder forever.

Duc du Clos

A doubt *is an imaginary shadow, which always leaves its reflections in the frame of the mind.*

Duc du Clos

When competitors *are not evenly comparable, competition itself is disqualified to be called so.*

Duc du Clos

Being alive *does not hurt much; it's living that's slowly killing me.*

Duc du Clos

Do it first, *it is often best to forget having done it, than having forgotten to do it.*

Duc du Clos

What one does *and gives as a living soul, will always be greater and better appreciated than what they do as a dying soul.*

Duc du Clos

It only takes *any man to lie, but a real man to admit it.*

Duc du Clos

A lie *is a temporary bandage, preventing a likely permanent scar to heal.*

Duc du Clos

At my age, *if I could only remember it, even without doing it, I'd be doing okay.*

Duc du Clos

It is acceptable, *even honorable, to have the freedom to fear than exulting a fear of freedom.*

Duc du Clos

Regardless *of the clearest explanation before our eyes, ignorance will always be the thickest blindfold we bear.*

Duc du Clos

Some people *drink trying to forget what drinking did to their remembrance the last time.*

Duc du Clos

The very best product *to ever have been invented for beauty, is the mirror.*

Duc du Clos

Rules *are like highways, we only follow them until we find the exit which leads us home.*

Duc du Clos

Turn *is a temporary positional possession of personal importance.*

Duc du Clos

One never seeks out *true inspiration. It always and simply finds one.*

Duc du Clos

An old bird *is still a bird. Even with blemished feathers and arthritic wingspan.*

Duc du Clos

Philosophy *is older than time: it is past, present and future. It is part of everything we are, anything we do, and whatever we think. Without philosophy, man would not harness the ideology to advance nor survive.*

Duc du Clos

If you are *happy and satisfied with simply "good", good luck. However, if you want to make "good" better, reach above it all, for the simplicity of satisfaction is only the ammunition to conquer greater success.*

Duc du Clos

The edge *is born out of the center and supported by the middle, however you look at it.*

Duc du Clos

Some horses run*, but a smart horse gallops.*

Duc du Clos

The true value *of our life is the dependency of another's.*

Duc du Clos

The importance *of a famous hand is valued only by the amount of times you have shaken it, for it loses its weight at every shake.*

Duc du Clos

An end *without a "d" is far to be endless.*

Duc du Clos

When you're *mean enough to do something bad enough, which you meant to do, apology is never good enough.*

Duc du Clos

Whoever is too concerned *and over interested in your yesterday, is someone who is not too comfortable inserting their present moment in your today, and has even greater doubts about your tomorrow.*

Duc du Clos

The past *is a treasure chest, which should guard and protect the days of its time.*

Duc du Clos

When one *treats others like dirt, keep in mind that it still has a greater volume than the dust we are all bound to become.*

Duc du Clos

While invisible, hesitation *is the tallest hurdle on your stride to success.*

Duc du Clos

It is not by chance *that the word opinion starts with the letter "O", for its also the shape and quantity of how much interest people have in it, if it's not theirs.*

Duc du Clos

No matter *how simultaneously two single items may appear to the sight, the mind infallibly always starts with one.*

Duc du Clos

Ambition *is by nature, a dormant beast sleeping with an open eye, which is easily awakened with the mere smell of opportunity.*

Duc du Clos

Most bad habits *are formed, not so often and so much out of constant repetitions, but out of repeated forgetfulness.*

Duc du Clos

Beauty *with little or no maintenance at all, is comfort at its purest form.*

Duc du Clos

While it's never *too late to start, don't rush two days at the time, but today is a very good time to start.*

Duc du Clos

Your life *should be one great shot at your own existence. If you have more than one, you are infringing in someone else's or you're simply having a mulligan.*

Duc du Clos

It is not *necessarily important to know a whole lot about anything, just a little bit about everything.*

Duc du Clos

If the past *is painful, it should be left exactly as what it is.*

Duc du Clos

A wound *never heals with perpetual picking of the scab.*

Duc du Clos

There may *be beauty and admiration in a poem that rhymes, but rarely sincerity, for it is then fabricated inspiration.*

Duc du Clos

You don't *necessarily have to be the best, just be better than you could ever have imagined, that in itself, is a great achievement.*

Duc du Clos

The norm *is overrated; it is best to be abnormally sane, than insanely normal.*

Duc du Clos

One is *not so much about the number, when others are weighed in to be next. It then becomes about the scale.*

Duc du Clos

In any endeavor, *the worst element you can lose is focus. Your best gain is perspective.*

Duc du Clos

The spirits of the souls, *which loved us, are often the stepping-stones on the path of our earthly journey.*

Duc du Clos

Talking about *people is as natural as eating; it should all be done in moderation. We don't want to regret what goes in our mouth, nor regret what comes out of it, for it's harder to retrieve what you said than going on a diet.*

Duc du Clos

Exhaling is a great opportunity to criticize someone, inhaling is a much greater and useful one to do it for oneself.

Duc du Clos

I confess, everything I ever lied about is all true.

Duc du Clos

Echo-nomy is a sound financial decision, which goes farther and gets bigger than its starting point.

Duc du Clos

Although *the rod may be yours, you'll never be an experienced fisherman if you can't understand that you are, at best, second to knowing when the fish has bitten.*

Duc du Clos

Life *is a beautiful painting; the people you choose to surround yourself should accomplish what a suitable frame would... compliment it without reservations.*

Duc du Clos

At any cost *some people will be red, even by the blood of others.*

Duc du Clos

When you *drag and play in the mud with others, your soles are no longer cleaner than theirs.*

Duc du Clos

A picture *used to speak a thousand words. Nowadays, a simple stroke or a click can mislead, depict or delete a million.*

Duc du Clos

Revenge and grudges are like little rivers and creeks. They dwindle down and perpetuate from one action to generations. The question is "who will be the bigger one acting as an ocean, ensuring that it all stops and ends here?"

Duc du Clos

Regrets are the natural characteristic flaws of every existence; a life without regrets is yet to be lived.

Duc du Clos

The truth *is an honest gift, which few people are worthy enough to deserve its revelation.*

Duc du Clos

Tomorrow *is a scale measuring today's acts.*

Duc du Clos

When you *are born in privileged hands, you don't really get to enjoy the village as others do.*

Duc du Clos

Watch your sermon, *children are life's best prophets and they will preach your words beyond the walls of your temple.*

Duc du Clos

It is a great notion *to aspire for success and a derision to be successfool.*

Duc du Clos

The truth *is like virgin water on a mountain: it flows gently, swiftly and most often on the same path without a thought. On the other hand, a lie is like a wave, forceful to overcome the shore, always changing and very unpredictable.*

Duc du Clos

Every morning *the day rises before you, be ready, for it will go on with or without you.*

Duc du Clos

One should *be proud of another and simply take pride in doing so.*

Duc du Clos

The reason *why the news is called so is because it is soon to be old.*

Duc du Clos

Governing *is not of physical strength, rather of mental abilities. So if a man believes in his mind, that a woman can't, he is yet to discover the location of the mind within his own anatomy.*

Duc du Clos

People *are born naturally innocent and gullible, it is in time they become callously stupid.*

Duc du Clos

In life there is always a whole lot of admiration to gain, the amount is up to you and based on the way you admire others.

Duc du Clos

Self-preparedness & self-awareness are self-protection against the many surprises of life.

Duc du Clos

I've been lucky that life followed me wherever I've been thus far.

Duc du Clos

As we judge others, we often fail to recognize that we are the basis from which we deduct our perceptions. If we were not aware of the existence of those perceptions, we may not have drawn their possibilities.

Duc du Clos

Our children will evolve and learn with or without us. It is in our best and intelligent interest to deviate them from their worst and most ignorant ones.

Duc du Clos

The mere request *of trust is the casting of a thicker veil on the face of the doubt.*

Duc du Clos

Rethink*, today's your newest day yet.*

Duc du Clos

Tick tock *by any and all means is a warning of time, not a tactic of time to make you lose its notion.*

Duc du Clos

There's a thin line between air of elegance and arrogance. People without the first always fear they are viewed as second rate, and call it pretention.

Duc du Clos

A diplomatic mind is like the air; it creates a custom atmosphere, eventually brings comfort, and undetectably escapes in diligent and appropriate time.

Duc du Clos

Even as normal becomes second nature, it will never necessarily mean natural.

Duc du Clos

If you have pride, you won't need to seek it in what you do, it will be self-evident.

Duc du Clos

Attempts to avoid one's shadow can only result in one's body bending out of shape.

Duc du Clos

If you teach *your daughter well enough, in her choice to the alter, you'll gain the son for whom you've long prayed.*

Duc du Clos

Literature *is the study of influential people you have never met, with the expectation to impress the people you may one day meet.*

Duc du Clos

Community is *a common familiar ground for past strangers, present neighbors, and forever friends.*

Duc du Clos

In order to dream big, *we need the patience to sleep soundly.*

Duc du Clos

Courtesy *is a rare virtue, which brings great joy at distribution.*

Duc du Clos

The little obvious *which is neglected, is an indication of greater coveted underlying details.*

Duc du Clos

Our tongues are the chisels which shape our relationship. Of our own hands we sculpture the good which we keep, or the unacceptable which we discard.

Duc du Clos

Things in life don't change, it is exactly the reason why we are created with the gift to change our own selves, which leads us to accommodate ourselves, as we believe things change.

Duc du Clos

The strong branches *we seek to eventually become are presently the fragile stems we are today.*

Duc du Clos

A good taste *often seeks fulfillment.*

Duc du Clos

An impression *is a founded thought or opinion, which is often based on profound misconceptions.*

Duc du Clos

We would appreciate *and enjoy one another much more, if the moment we chose to judge someone's flaws, it triggers a reflection in our own mirror to face ours.*

Duc du Clos

As the wheel *of time turns, the two worst things one can do is stand on its path or hold on to its spokes. It is always wiser to follow and glide, as one eases on down behind its track.*

Duc du Clos

The untainted truth only comes out over the lips of innocence.

Duc du Clos

Even of the driest well, when well thought out, it eventually offers a new alternative and purpose.

Duc du Clos

It is always lonely to live in your own world.

Duc du Clos

I have always lived under the premise that the world was simply round, until *I* witnessed the sharp angles and the corners society cut to change it's shape.

Duc du Clos

Diplomacy is not taking a hatchet blindly to your words, disregarding the knots of its grain, rather carefully chiseling them as a sculptor would.

Duc du Clos

Even of our best dispositions, our position in life only offers four cardinal points.

Duc du Clos

One's self control and respect should always outweigh another's fear.

Duc du Clos

Pride is simply the result from the struggle between shame and humiliation.

Duc du Clos

In life, *it is in doing the unnecessary that we often capture a better way to do what we'll need to do in time of necessity.*

Duc du Clos

We often ask *the impossible of ourselves, because of the constant intent to reach higher than our mind offers.*

Duc du Clos

Only in *our dark hours do we seek forgiveness, forgetting that it is much easier to find what you're looking for in the dark, if you knew its shape in the light of the day.*

Duc du Clos

If you can *assess, recognize and accept your faults, your success will be twice as easy.*

Duc du Clos

If the evidence *of a man's worth is his assaults or insults, in his mind, his value can only be surpassed by his own ignorance.*

Duc du Clos

Mediocrity *is the manual result of a mindless job done heartlessly.*

Duc du Clos

The mere *fact that one wants to express it does not change the fact itself. Only the occurrence of a factual event can create or alter facts.*

Duc du Clos

It is often in respecting oneself, that we can clearly demonstrate respect for others. Some other time, we should trust the mirror.

Duc du Clos

If you can't imagine it, you won't attempt it. If you won't attempt it, it won't happen, even in your imagination.

Duc du Clos

The book of experience has no pages, but a lifelong lesson.

Duc du Clos

Eating one's last handful of seed rather than planting it, is eating one's last meal.

Duc du Clos

Having the ability to dispossess someone of the object of your jealousy is not a disposition for the mind to enter.

Duc du Clos

Even when your world crumbles, keep in mind that you are still its foundation, and use that experience to trust that it is nature's way… a gift to help you architect your own vision on stronger, more modern structure.

Duc du Clos

The best weapon *in defying ignorance is to challenge knowledge.*

Duc du Clos

A good gesture *is not a sign of consideration; only consideration at its consistency should be viewed as a sign of good virtue.*

Duc du Clos

The ability *to feel guilty is an honor, of which any good soul should feel proud.*

Duc du Clos

Aristocracy *is the art of good fortune.*

Duc du Clos

You can't be *right doing wrong and you can't be wrong doing right.*

Duc du Clos

With financial freedom, *one can buy school not class, for you'll always be its prisoner.*

Duc du Clos

Security *is the insulation of any relationship.*

Duc du Clos

A diamond, *to contrary belief, is not a sign of love, rather a glare of attraction, which brings one closer to inspect the clarity of one's relationship.*

Duc du Clos

The truth, *in which one does not believe, may be an indication of one's actual value beyond the realm of their expectation of you, and that is satisfying.*

Duc du Clos

The comfort *in what we know should be approached with confidence; the fear of the new and the unknown should be faced with caution and defiance.*

Duc du Clos

Bad things *will surely happen on their own. But good things only happen when you make them.*

Duc du Clos

When you *are a parent, you have to understand that the offer of freedom is no substitute for love.*

Duc du Clos

Certainty *is a warm blanket in the chilling cold of doubt.*

Duc du Clos

Another difference between elegance and arrogance is that, the first does not necessarily need the second to feel complete. While the second believes it needs the first to be whole.

Duc du Clos

One's own personal idea for the future is the blueprint and the foundation, which life uses for the structure of one's tomorrow.

Duc du Clos

There will often be rules, but if you are the exception, there will always be you.

Duc du Clos

Respect is like a seed. Plant a little and it will grow a lot.

Duc du Clos

Hope is a corner you pray you can turn, while wishing for better things at its bend.

Duc du Clos

Impressions *are formed on past visual experiences and created on present imaginary feelings and sense of deduction.*

Duc du Clos

There can never be *true protection without the fear of punishment.*

Duc du Clos

Life *is a 220V outlet, when powered, will allow one to plug in and enjoy a variety of appliances of one's dreams.*

Duc du Clos

Love *is a variable in the fraction of living. It changes with admiration and the applications of affection.*

Duc du Clos

Our mind *is a simple puddle, with the proper stimulant, can create a splash of a tsunami.*

Duc du Clos

Patience *is a drop of time in the goblet of life. The more cautiously it is poured, the safer it reaches its volume.*

Duc du Clos

There is *the fortunate rich, who wastes his present life, living poorly, as there is the misfortunate poor, who destroys his future seeking riches.*

Duc du Clos

The equation of Life:
Complexion **+** *Education* **−** *Economic Situation* **÷** *Religion* **x** *Luck* **=** *LIFE*

Duc du Clos

Standard is the measurement of living. Your life will be out of proportion if you ignore its value.

Duc du Clos

Regret is a load, which should impede your heels, rather than your toes.

Duc du Clos

The title, which is acquired by admiration, will always surpass the appreciation obtained by titles.

Duc du Clos

Physics *is not a science, but it is of course, a natural fact. Where mathematics is the science, formulating itself to also cover and discern such natural phenomenon.*

Duc du Clos

The questions *you are asked are never intended for your benefit, as you already know the answers. Too often, it is to satisfy another's curiosity.*

Duc du Clos

Insecurity *is a possible opinion of yourself, which you fearfully believe is formulated in the mind of others.*

Duc du Clos

Lucky is the one *who already is, hopeful is the one who seeks to be, while hopeless is the one who does not believe in either.*

Duc du Clos

We are all *only halfway happy, until we understand that pure and total happiness is 50% fact, 40% faith and 10% fiction.*

Duc du Clos

There's aggression *and there's strength. Aggression is an uncontrollable emotion, which often overwhelms the mind; while strength is the power at will of the mind.*

Duc du Clos

Self-respect *is a shield, meshed out of behavioral actions to help form from others, one's own opinion.*

Duc du Clos

Our accomplishments *would have been greater if time would wait, as we make plans for reaching them.*

Duc du Clos

Your own respect *is weighed, based on the scale upon which you set another's.*

Duc du Clos

The earth *may be round, but the world is far to be, for it has many angles.*

Duc du Clos

What you have heard, seen, or thought of someone, are simply inadequate contents for their evaluation.

Duc du Clos

The misconception between self-confidence and arrogance is largely due to people lacking the first and somehow possessing too much of the latter.

Duc du Clos

The attempt *of grandiosity resulting in catastrophe always doubles its failure.*

Duc du Clos

When given *the choice, a thirst should be quenched from the fountain with the sweetest drink.*

Duc du Clos

The efforts *put forth today are the preventative measures from the failures of tomorrow.*

Duc du Clos

Naturally, *we all view the unknown through the lens of fear. However, it should not be captured as an impediment, rather an opportunity to click and snap a better picture of a successful achievement.*

Duc du Clos

A niche *is, after all, a nest, a sheltering habitat constructed over time out of patience and love; therefore, no one can ever find his own niche, for it will always be someone else's castle.*

Duc du Clos

The true value *of a real man is not measured by the level of pain he inflicts on another, rather the level of compassion he displays towards anyone hurt, by yet another half man.*

Duc du Clos

Bleak curiosity *of strangers is to discern your placement on the shelves of society.*

Duc du Clos

It is less affective *to experience failure on the way to the top, than failing and falling from the top.*

Duc du Clos

Regret *is just like stacking up empty cans in the pantry of your minds, taking valuable space from the basket of joy the present could bring.*

Duc du Clos

The greatest *and truest legacy is not the imprints on the path we left behind, rather the planned map for the journey ahead.*

Duc du Clos

When one *does not pay cash, one never feels the blood gushing out of the cut until the end of the month, when the knife is pulled out… to make a new incision.*

Duc du Clos

Fortunately, *the value of the greatest treasures can never be validated by sight.*

Duc du Clos

What one possesses *in abundance never makes up for what one lacks.*

Duc du Clos

The limit *on the distant horizon, where the sight ends, begins the doubtful appreciation of the imagination.*

Duc du Clos

A single string *can't be braided. It's only by intertwining, can we collectively find the strength to weave the rope, which will pull us to safety from ourselves.*

Duc du Clos

When and if *you truly love your children to death, you, at a certain point, had to have, at the very least, liked the other mate to a simple malady.*

Duc du Clos

Feelings *are strange and timely emotions…*

… like love at first sight
… gradual disconnection
… periodic illusions
… momentary lapse of disappointment
… temporary affection
… instant disapproval
… and constant tribulations
… to the point of forever new beginnings.

Duc du Clos

Whoever attempts to assure you in not worrying about a situation, has already and fully assessed the reasons why you could, and maybe should.

Duc du Clos

A poet is an artist who uses ink to paint the many shapes and shades of emotions.

Duc du Clos

Amongst friends, understand that good times will be reminisced upon once in a while. Remember however, the hurtful behavior will constantly linger and live on forever.

Duc du Clos

Someone who's too focused about what they have done in the past has a present handicap, which will impede, if not paralyze his future.

Duc du Clos

When in necessity, seek with laborious effort, dignity and honesty. When in possession, act humbly, and gratefully with unlimited altruism.

Duc du Clos

Improvement *is a natural process of repetitive acts, which transcend into experience.*

Duc du Clos

One may lie *a great deal. However, the truth is even greater, for it is one's honest existence.*

Duc du Clos

Never critique *any situation, if you can't cure, or at the very least, improve its malady.*

Duc du Clos

In seeking 100%, *if you fail half way, embrace the assurance in knowing that you will never have to fail 100%, and it should be a great incentive to continue reaching for success.*

Duc du Clos

Any explosive *news of fashion will eventually settle along with the dust that it caused, within its last microscopic grain.*

Duc du Clos

Ignorance *is the mountain from which we extract the rock we believe to be our knowledge. It is however, with excessive knowledge, can we crumble ignorance to a pebble.*

Duc du Clos

To simply *and fairly count, one has to start by one. Any other grouping or combination is, at the very least, an addition.*

Duc du Clos

Fears of bitterness *or pettiness can only blur and impede your vision of success.*

Duc du Clos

Your shadow *is your soul. The first day you don't see it, will be the second day of the last time you will have seen it, and by then, you won't miss it until it's far gone.*

Duc du Clos

Where you are *from, affects the way you are perceived. Where you are, influences the way you are viewed. Where you are going, dictates the way you are pursued.*

Duc du Clos

You may be born lucky enough to even think you're also smart. But intelligence is learned.

Duc du Clos

To be truly happy, one has to understand that there is more to one's existence than one's own life.

Duc du Clos

You can't have peace of mind if your mind is made of pieces.

Duc du Clos

The gotten impression *is the given one. So only offer what you really want to give.*

Duc du Clos

The deception *of a lie, weighs much more on the mind of the believing recipient for the fact they feel they have been had.*

Duc du Clos

Your destination *should never be altered by your departure.*

Duc du Clos

Often time, *a lie is a shield of self-preservation, reflecting from the mirror of self-presumed acceptation.*

Duc du Clos

Dismissing an issue *at first breath is often the only exercise of a lazy tongue.*

Duc du Clos

Regardless of all else, one must believe the man, whom *I* said *I* am, is the man whom *I* know to be.

Duc du Clos

If one doesn't know the value of shame, one will never truly formulate the value of pride.

Duc du Clos

A habit is a natural practice, which eventually becomes practically natural.

Duc du Clos

Regardless *of one's success, until one comprehends methodically the mechanism of execution in accomplishment, one can't pass it on, for it is yet to be a method.*

Duc du Clos

When people *are above you, they don't really care to take you down. It is only when it is hard for them to see over your shoulder that your height becomes a hurdle.*

Duc du Clos

The credit of others one unfairly garnishes is a debt to ones self in the transaction of life.

Duc du Clos

The truth is not necessarily what you say, rather what is believed to have been said.

Duc du Clos

The experience you've gained is for you to live and others to enjoy. So pass it on.

Duc du Clos

We may not choose our children. But we only need to see their own choices to be proud of the choice we have ourselves made in having them.

Duc du Clos

Design the present well enough to make a planned past out of the future.

Duc du Clos

What good is life, when the "o's" are not shared to the point of God.

Duc du Clos

Intelligence *is the ability to come up with common solutions in extraordinary moments when the common mind fails to do so.*

Duc du Clos

Relief *from your sufferance can only be appeased in the forgiveness of your perpetrators.*

Duc du Clos

A thirsty lip drinks from the first drop of water, while the leisured lip seeks the freshest drop of water.

Duc du Clos

A smart farmer who plans to successfully sell his crop, plants friendship first, then his produce.

Duc du Clos

Your conscience is your shadow. You can evade it only for a glance as you turn the corner of your character.

Duc du Clos

There's no *long future in one's asset if one's asset is one's feature, for only the mind is everlasting.*

Duc du Clos

The world *may be a bitter place, it's up to us to treat it well to become a better place.*

Duc du Clos

Don't litter the *liters for they can be a gallon of weight on the needless paper trail of our planet.*

Duc du Clos

An indestructible heart *is either out of reach or made of stone. Either way, it lacks the joy and pleasure of another witnessing its beating.*

Duc du Clos

The sequence *of extreme living has its existential consequences.*

Duc du Clos

It is sometimes *uncommonly wise to know someone you trust, than to trust someone you know.*

Duc du Clos

Life will always *have very little to offer to those who don't value it as a good fortune.*

Duc du Clos

Often time, *luck, the greatest gift of all, becomes the delegate of fate in the convoy of good.*

Duc du Clos

You don't leave your past behind by burning the bridges you have crossed. You only make it more difficult to get back to it in time of need.

Duc du Clos

The assumption of knowing the truth is an artificial glare, which will fade as the real fact hits you at its natural angle.

Duc du Clos

Ambition *often hides behind the mask of greed to partake in the masquerade of life.*

Duc du Clos

In any desperate *attempt to disguise the truth, the lie often stands surprisingly plain in that masquerade.*

Duc du Clos

Good business *is providing what the customer needs, while promoting what they believe they want.*

Duc du Clos

Sometimes *the darkness offers a clearer path than the brightest light, which may, in retrospect blind you.*

Duc du Clos

Tomorrow *is our refuge of salvation under permanent construction; every ill deed today is the removal of a valuable stone within its foundation.*

Duc du Clos

Jealousy is like a weed, not necessarily planted, not exactly wanted, yet it is only good to choke the other beautiful living organisms surrounding it.

Duc du Clos

The moment you stop caring about the world, it can't help but instantaneously reciprocate.

Duc du Clos

One should never raise, nor praise the glory of another, at the crumbling risk of one's own foundation.

Duc du Clos

Pride is the chisel which shapes your character, while shame is the mallet without which, the pressure would always be in the palm of your hand.

Duc du Clos

No problem is borne without a solution. We simply over focus on its resolution, overlooking to which problem the solution belongs, thus creating a problematic situation.

Duc du Clos

A river *never really runs dry. For the moment it no longer fulfills its purpose by running to the sea, it is indeed no longer a river.*

Duc du Clos

The moment *you start feeling comfortable in your stretched skin, it is then the time to worry about its marks.*

Duc du Clos

Paranoid *is one of the many excuses we manifest in accusing others of thoughts we actually feel about ourselves.*

Duc du Clos

Consideration *is the corresponding effort made in matching someone else's comfort or sentiment.*

Duc du Clos

Happiness *at its magnitude is the little drop of joy you bring to the life of another.*

Duc du Clos

The person *next to you, with whom you don't care to share a word, may eventually be the one to write your life's story.*

Duc du Clos

Pride *is a positive molecule while shame is negative. Remember, when your nerves need electricity or electrodes to operate, they can't have one without the other.*

Duc du Clos

One book *can be borne out of mere inspiration; the next may be out of shear desperation and clear perspiration.*

Duc du Clos

Only a fool *misconstrues a string of hair for a rope of power, for there is always a chain of command.*

Duc du Clos

Learning *is a present sacrifice of the mind for the future comfort of the body.*

Duc du Clos

Power begins *by one's ambition and ends with the deception of many.*

Duc du Clos

Curiosity *will always be worth its satisfaction, for it's less expensive to spend any amount on finding out at once, than a fortune on wondering forever.*

Duc du Clos

Nobody should be *empowered to alter another's sentiments, nor moments.*

Duc du Clos

When a soul *suffers by your hands, your own fate will be in others.*

Duc du Clos

Necessity *naturally will always outweigh its load.*

Duc du Clos

Satisfaction *may be visible to others, but integrity will always be a warm light that glows inside.*

Duc du Clos

Weight *is like an old heavy and dusty raggedy coat. You won't have to take it off, if you don't put it on.*

Duc du Clos

If you *are content evaluating yourself on how far you have been by where you are, your journey has then just begun.*

Duc du Clos

As long as *we behave as sheep, the shepherd will always flock us up in groups.*

Duc du Clos

Credit yourself *of being great, when and only when no one else can be trained to do what you naturally can.*

Duc du Clos

Much more *importance to you I would have, if about me, nothing else you knew, but my name.*

Duc du Clos

Opportunity *will always be life's mystery staircase. If you skip a step or two, you'll never know how high you could have gone, or how low you could have stumbled, for certainty is a step-by-step process.*

Duc du Clos

We are not dumb, *we simply fear to develop and use our intelligence wisely.*

Duc du Clos

Consequence *is the only constant, yet ever changing situation.*

Duc du Clos

As a husband*, one should believe oneself to be the perfect wife.*

Duc du Clos

We keep complaining about the gap, the inequality, the difference and unfairness of the world. Those are exactly the components making it spin on itself. Who knows? As it turns, those with their heads held up too high will be upside down.

Duc du Clos

***If you can't** summon your conscience to witness the making of a decision, it is then not worth reaching.*

Duc du Clos

***The judge** may wear the robe, however the robe does not make a judge.*

Duc du Clos

***Neither the collar** nor the cloth can be valid testaments for the Priest.*

Duc du Clos

The only time money can buy peace of mind is when clear and good conscience was the derivative of its acquisition.

Duc du Clos

Diplomacy is understanding that one can indubitably defeat one's enemy at first strike and yet passionately still seeks peaceful truce.

Duc du Clos

The tailor *may invariable make the suit, yet the suit does not necessarily make the tailor.*

Duc du Clos

A non-studious mind *may feel that degree is best left alone to room temperature, until it steps out into the real cold world.*

Duc du Clos

Pride *cannot be bought. But once lost, the price to regain it doubles.*

Duc du Clos

The history *one should care most about should start today.*

Duc du Clos

The first step *in going further is to recognize your limit.*

Duc du Clos

The best strategic plan *in exceeding is realizing at what speed you've been traveling.*

Duc du Clos

Validation *of others should come from within, otherwise, it's simply influence from others.*

Duc du Clos

In life, *if you're not a bit goofy, you're breathing too seriously.*

Duc du Clos

Depression *is a dark cloud which can easily be dissipated by small drops of determination.*

Duc du Clos

Be consumed *in diversity and you're on your path to a beautiful rainbow, otherwise you'll eventually be cornered in a grey area as time goes by.*

Duc du Clos

Interest *is dividends based on how little someone knows of you. Once satisfied, the bond is gone. Like stocks, they'll split and merge onto someone new.*

Duc du Clos

Even a twig *knows life is too short to grow old into one direction, so branch out and live a little.*

Duc du Clos

Society *is a human scale which can too easily be tipped by a simple financial glow.*

Duc du Clos

In life, *the sincere path one creates with good friends is invisible to enemies to follow.*

Duc du Clos

225

Prepositions are like cars, if you don't know how to use them, they can't go "from" anywhere "to" nowhere, and you'll always get into at least small incidents.

Duc du Clos

It is so much easier to make loud fanfare to disguise one's talent than to play soft melody, which may display clear inadequacies.

Duc du Clos

In giving it all, one should always find enough energy not just to win, but savor victory.

Duc du Clos

When you find yourself in your enemy's backyard, a friendship has suddenly died or foolishness is born.

Duc du Clos

If you sincerely and fervently pray to the spirit you believe in, yours won't carry the burden of life alone.

Duc du Clos

The willingness *to achieve a goal is already 50% accomplishment towards its success.*

Duc du Clos

If we walk *towards kingdom majestically, on the throne we'll sit. Any other way, by its sides, we'll stand.*

Duc du Clos

To have *a final thought in any situation is ultimately one of the greatest gifts that life can ever offer.*

Duc du Clos

A deviated thought *from the truth is not necessarily a lie. It is however, the distorted beginning of either one.*

Duc du Clos

Arrogance *will often start a war. Bravery will always fervently defend in battles, but only true courage can win the war.*

Duc du Clos

Pity on someone else is just the shadow of the magnificent compassion you physically bore within yourself.

Duc du Clos

The only good thing about ignorance is that it's a disease one can treat oneself.

Duc du Clos

Void of a conscience, even a good mind resembling a beautiful flower, is nothing but a weed in the end.

Duc du Clos

***A true artisan** crafts his art for a lifetime, yet finds his muse, only once in his lifetime.*

Duc du Clos

***To be invincible** is not in the absence of defeat, but in the thought of its impossibility.*

Duc du Clos

***Self-preservation** does not need to take shape at the destruction of others.*

Duc du Clos

The family *is the land where love's born, blooms and grows.*

Duc du Clos

Too often, *our behavior is the instrument we provide others for our own demise.*

Duc du Clos

The displaying of gold *is merely a sign of possession, not necessarily of one's worthiness.*

Duc du Clos

If you believe today to be the worst day of your life… for simple comfort, just imagine the improvement on tomorrow.

Duc du Clos

Jealousy is like a child's imagination running wild. If not tamed, it will take the shape of a monster which could easily devour and savor a good relationship.

Duc du Clos

Indecision is not necessarily a sign of confusion, rather that of a mind which believes in more options than those present.

Duc du Clos

Fortune may or may not be a blessing. Blessings however, are certainly great fortunes.

Duc du Clos

The value you have should mirror the value you are.

Duc du Clos

Every era has its error.   The difference is the risk of the era, and the gravity of the error, as they control the speed of evolution.

Duc du Clos

Don't just leave your life in a will.   Give yourself a present by living in the now, for tomorrow belongs to history to come.

Duc du Clos

Unlike fortune, *importance and respect can't be inherited.*

Duc du Clos

Respect *is the frame and core of importance.*

Duc du Clos

A sheltered *and ignored mind will eventually need an exposed and educated one for ultimate protection.*

Duc du Clos

History *should always and only be the foundation, not the roof, nor ceiling of the structure in which we progress and live.*

Duc du Clos

The stranger, *with whom you share the pavement today, may be the companion, with whom you'll share another path on the journey that's life.*

Duc du Clos

Respect *is the simplest grain of great abundance. Sow a little, harvest a lot.*

Duc du Clos

Consideration is *the mother of all virtues.*

Duc du Clos

Too much *of a single good thing cannot be all that good.*

Duc du Clos

We have to learn *to be a little conceited so as not to concede in the struggles of life.*

Duc du Clos

Life's too short *to walk too tall. For it will be harder to look at it in the eye, and sincerely ask for forgiveness.*

Duc du Clos

One who always thinks *nothing matters, may not have much of it in the brain.*

Duc du Clos

Someone's body language *is the translation of his scripted character.*

Duc du Clos

Exaggeration *is the assured limit of exactitude.*

Duc du Clos

You can never *appreciate nor evaluate the softness and the warmth of the sand, if not barefoot you walk.*

Duc du Clos

Appearance is a visual which resonates much louder than its verbal expression.

Duc du Clos

Beauty is a universal recognition; anything else is personal taste or opinion.

Duc du Clos

If you are allergic to my flowers, don't let your tears drop on their petals, for they as well may be to you.

Duc du Clos

One's life *is a magnify-scent vast, wild and beautiful garden. When living it, embellish it as if creating a bouquet in a magnificent vase. As long as the flowers are yours, rearrange them the way you please.*

Duc du Clos

Don't let *circumstance create the time you spend with your family. It has enough help and opportunity, so architect your own.*

Duc du Clos

Maturity *is a raging river one can traverse only by the canoe of experience.*

Duc du Clos

Appearance *is a judgment, which requires no basis, nor facts to substantiate its entry into a mind opened to the wrong conclusion.*

Duc du Clos

To the mind *out of any of its own, success is a simple word with excessive lettering.*

Duc du Clos

Your reputation *is like an egg. Once broken, your choices are limited. Deviled eggs or egg salad are definitely out of the equation. So don't leave your reputation spoil on the back burner.*

Duc du Clos

A good judge *has to admire himself when he sees the kind of lawyer he could have been, as he judges those who daily approach his bench.*

Duc du Clos

The hand *which did not take the time to plant any seed, will have only time in hand to regret as it weeds.*

Duc du Clos

All men *are created equal, but as life goes on it all changes, for there will be thieves among us to mix up the equation.*

Duc du Clos

In life, *there's always room for improvement, in art always room for improvisation.*

Duc du Clos

The bamboo *is light because it's hollow inside. It is strong because it is flexible. So don't be full of the unnecessary and rigid to the single shape of a narrow mind.*

Duc du Clos

Don't judge *your friends' true character on the basis of the way they treat you… rather in that of which they treat others. For their natural instinct won't be influenced by any bias of friendship.*

Duc du Clos

The ink *may be man-made blood, but it can naturally hurt as it dictates the fate of another.*

Duc du Clos

An artist *never has the luxury of an admitted mistake, only new discovery in progress.*

Duc du Clos

The bearer of bad news *always thinks of his as an important tongue.*

Duc du Clos

If you start *working your way up from the middle, you can only inspire half he people. The rest will either think you cheated or had it made.*

Duc du Clos

My mother *used to say true inspiration is like corn. The shape it enters your mind is the shape it will exit. Fortunately, mine was off the cob.*

Duc du Clos

***Without consideration,** no act is ever committed, no success is ever reached. Otherwise, it is simply a mere accident.*

Duc du Clos

***If your elbows** and shoulders keep knocking on others', your high horse is not that much taller nor faster.*

Duc du Clos

***Art** is an inspiration. Inspiration is improvisation. Improvisation is necessity by design, or art in need.*

Duc du Clos

Life *is like a beautiful and personal picture; the people with whom you surround yourself are the frame, which dictates its value.*

Duc du Clos

Mere divulgence *should never be the sacrificial wine selected to quench the thirst of a stranger's curiosity.*

Duc du Clos

Imagination is an endless journey, a path on which one should blindly find joy and relentlessly travel.

Duc du Clos

No one owes any other explanation to anyone but the truth; anything else is a lie.

Duc du Clos

Only a fool judges a calm man by his actions, for it can all be calculated.

Duc du Clos

A hurtful truth is like a toothache. Although it will bring you relief after admission, the excruciating pain of extraction always outweighs the consequence of living with it a little longer everyday.

Duc du Clos

Honesty is required only when fairness is expected of all parties involved. If you don't believe me, go ask the other two Kings of the Orient.

Duc du Clos

Money *may not bring you "peace of mind", but it does bring you "piece of mine".*

Duc du Clos

Courage *is a beast needing to be constantly fed.*

Duc du Clos

The beginning *sometimes has to rely on the end for a secure and calculated start.*

Duc du Clos

Happiness *is sacrificing oneself without questioning where the "y" used to be, and still be contented, as the word happy itself.*

Duc du Clos

Humiliation *is a suffering act, from which, one should draw humility at its purest form in order to become humble in return.*

Duc du Clos

Tears of bitterness *or pity can only blur and impede your vision of success.*

Duc du Clos

While playing the game of life*, mistakes should be the exception, not the norm.*

Duc du Clos

It only takes *a single stroke to fix the IMPOSSIBLE! With the stroke of an apostrophe, "I" ' "M" possible! (I'm Possible)*

Duc du Clos

Perception *is the formula of adjustments, an ever-changing variable of equations… rearranging your plan as the action occurs.*

Duc du Clos

I can *fix everything but my life, for to do so, I'd have to step out of it in order to capture the whole picture.*

Duc du Clos

Only a lie *needs to be a production, the simplistic truth needs not be sophisticated.*

Duc du Clos

Old friends *who become enemies should understand that what you no longer have, should not have more importance than what you used to, however little it was. For "good old friends" will always be better than "bad, new enemies".*

Duc du Clos

It's much easier *for some people to be vegetarians rather than humanitarians. Yet, it is a shorter distance to care about who lives next door, than what lives in the wild.*

Duc du Clos

Regret *is a repentant emotion, which can be felt only when it is too late; up until then it's called stupidity.*

Duc du Clos

We may *be creatures of habit, but habits are small creatures of their own… if constantly fed, will become untamed beasts.*

Duc du Clos

Implications *are very misleading, for the exposed or expressed facts may be misconstrued.*

Duc du Clos

If you think I imply and you infer, we might be on the same page of two different books.

Duc du Clos

When painting a story, the brush with the thicker stroke will always paint a louder picture.

Duc du Clos

In families' views, one has to make responsibility a priority.

Duc du Clos

Being mediocre *is as practical as being invisible, for to be recognized, one has to be the best or the worst.*

Duc du Clos

Being *a true and fair human being is caring about everyone on any sphere, not just the "at most".*

Duc du Clos

Any moment *of Eureka for one is a moment of burial for another, for the agony of searching is over.*

Duc du Clos

As you wake up, *pray at least once and do at least one extraordinary thing. In return, it will be as normal and ordinary as it was meant to be.*

Duc du Clos

Life should *be an enjoyable existence, or it is simply being lived.*

Duc du Clos

Power *is like fortune; the more you abuse it, the less of it you have left.*

Duc du Clos

A business transaction *is like the tossing of a coin; only by illusion can both parties be winners.*

Duc du Clos

Words which float on the mind, should never be as light on the tongue, for their delivery shall display reasonable consideration.

Duc du Clos

Repetition builds memorization, which transcends into recollection to form education… the temple of defined knowledge.

Duc du Clos

We are all humans, *so we should pray not to prey.*

Duc du Clos

The weight *of a spoken word is always heavier than that of a thought, for it has the ton of a sound.*

Duc du Clos

For some people, *secondary means it is not the first "ary", missing what's necessary in making it first, as in primary.*

Duc du Clos

No judgment should even be contemplated while consideration is so one sided that the other is ignored.

Duc du Clos

Being a writer, sometimes at night one single word can keep one up, and it does not necessarily have to be "awake".

Duc du Clos

In order to acquire self-preservation, one has to first develop self-evaluation.

Duc du Clos

A lie *is what you believe it to be, not what it necessarily is until it is discovered to be so.*

Duc du Clos

A lone contented *and satisfied worker will always outperform a dozen disgruntled ones.*

Duc du Clos

Incentive *is the direct fuel to success and accomplishment.*

Duc du Clos

Some authors don't read another poets quotes or adages, not so much for fear of plagiarism, rather for the disliking of motto.cycling.

Duc du Clos

Tomorrow is absolutely nothing without today, as much as "ception" is without a prefix: as in reception, perception, interception, inception and deception etc.

Duc du Clos

Suspicion *is a dirty surrealistic brush, which can cast shadows of doubts on the most realistic and clearest canvas.*

Duc du Clos

An intelligent horse *will always chose to be led and guided by its harness, rather than its mane.*

Duc du Clos

The joy *of a great mind is the intelligent journey of a daily learning.*

Duc du Clos

Sometimes it's better to *have an old dog drag its tail throughout its journey than having a young puppy sniff its way to find its destination.*

Duc du Clos

There may *not be anything unusual about the common thing, but there could be something uncommon about the usual thing, such as love.*

Duc du Clos

One should *learn the distinct difference between fear and respect. While one may fear another whom they don't respect, one can still respect someone they fear.*

Duc du Clos

We all *have values. They are simply circumstantial.*

Duc du Clos

Home court *advantage is just that. Not a secure and certain victory.*

Duc du Clos

As one manipulates the truth, *one can't help but automatically and instantly feel trapped in the dark labyrinth of lies… as only admission and apologies are the steps on the ladder, leading to higher, brighter, and safer ground.*

Duc du Clos

A quote *... is like a painting, a bed of lilies by watercolor. Explanation becomes the rain, as every word is a droplet distorting its beauty.*

Duc du Clos

A friend *is at the very least, a stranger who has, in time, acquired the benefit of the doubt, and until the end, the entitlement of even a vague explanation.*

Duc du Clos

No one knows what *one takes personally, which is what makes the word so individually worthwhile.*

Duc du Clos

Anyone *with a reason to will lie.*

Duc du Clos

Hatred *is a contagious bacterial sentiment, which often grows simply by breathing on others around you.*

Duc du Clos

The mere presence *of illegal substance in the mind is the absolute absence of common sense in the brain.*

Duc du Clos

Though they may mitigate your sentence, personal circumstances are never good enough reasons to ignore, nor break the law.

Duc du Clos

Doubt is what makes us certain that we don't know for sure.

Duc du Clos

Simply knowing that you know that I know, is all I need to know, that you know that I know.

Duc du Clos

Fear is not fact. *It is simply fiction in its imaginary form. It is so called because it is yet to manifest itself into fact, however unrealistic.*

Duc du Clos

Art *is vulnerably powerful.*

Duc du Clos

The restricted room of ignorance *will always seem larger than the endless hallway of knowledge leading to the tunnel of understanding.*

Duc du Clos

If you live in an environment, which does not affect you, in it you don't belong.

Duc du Clos

Consideration is not at all about leverage with others, rather alleviation for others in their moments of need.

Duc du Clos

A lie has to have a close enough resemblance to the truth to disguise and pass itself as such.

Duc du Clos

My hands hold the power *of the wind, and as it blows, the breeze you feel through your hair is the sensation of my fingers between every strand.*

Duc du Clos

Embarrassment *is credit to no one. The thoughtless feels selfishly good just for a short while, as the subjected feels badly for a long while.*

Duc du Clos

Most friends *are enemies with nothing on you.*

Duc du Clos

Some people *are close friends because their dagger won't reach as far as your sword.*

Duc du Clos

A very good and long time friend, *whom you have only known by a first name, is less likely to become your enemy.*

Duc du Clos

Fortune *is a mountain where I keep stubbing my toe on the very first stone below.*

Duc du Clos

A writer *has a story and always seeks an end. The poet's end always seeks a story.*

Duc du Clos

Revelation *is a tempestuous storm, which never leaves the ship on its original drafted destination.*

Duc du Clos

People are like seasons, *"weather" you like them or not, you'll meet them all, and eventually, once in a while, one will more than make up for the regrettable others.*

Duc du Clos

Courtesy *often glides on the smooth slope of cooperation, while rudeness always stumbles on the rocky road of alienation.*

Duc du Clos

Money should not *be the salary of life, rather an added bonus for a life well lived, fairly and generously.*

Duc du Clos

The hurtful pleasantry *of a friend in good times is a verbal rehearsal of much worse to come on the stage of your friendship.*

Duc du Clos

Some people move *to certain zip codes because of an inferiority complex, which ultimately develops into an illusion of superiority.*

Duc du Clos

Love does not need to be a fanfare; it only needs to be whispered with a sincere heart.

Duc du Clos

A wife will often stand beside you. A wife who loves you will always stand behind you.

Duc du Clos

A friend who speaks neither well nor ill of you is silent evidence of a forever friend.

Duc du Clos

Sacrifice is an act of true selflessness; otherwise, it would be a selfish obligation.

Duc du Clos

Philosophy is the art of making and understanding a whole lot out of nothing at all.

Duc du Clos

A tree without roots is simply a weak pole at the mercy of the breeze.

Duc du Clos

How, in Heaven, *will we behave when the place of others we won't assign and ours humbly we'll have to occupy.*

Duc du Clos

Sometimes we disturb *the entire life of our brothers for a single day of passing fancy, while we, with less fear and concern in our hearts, prepare to ascend to our ultimate destination.*

Duc du Clos

A translator *can translate your words all day without, for a single moment, capturing and conveying your sentiments.*

Duc du Clos

Regardless of time *of awakening, one's day does not begin until one prays.*

Duc du Clos

An artist *must I be, to become any king's envy.*

Duc du Clos

My sons, *I'm so very proud of you today… that any future accomplishments you may accumulate tomorrow will simply be mere pedestals for the pure symbolic stature of pride you are to me at this present moment.*

Duc du Clos

Scandals are the late ceremonies celebrated by those who were not initially invited.

Duc du Clos

Love does not need to be fair, it only needs to be true.

Duc du Clos

A wild imagination is the fruit of a lively and restless mind.

Duc du Clos

I express myself because I exist. I exist because I feel. I feel because of the emotions in my existence, so I express myself by the few words I need, because I feel that my emotions exist.

Duc du Clos

If with your tongue you caress the words you express, like sweet massage, they will glide on the lobes through the canal of appreciation.

Duc du Clos

You only have two hands and life is short. So hold on fast to only what matters and let it feel the grip of your embrace.

Duc du Clos

The sadness in growing old *is not that one can't envision nor face the future, for not much of it is left… rather one will lose the capacity to remember the past and its wondrous memories, which made us smile.*

Duc du Clos

Adages, Proverbs

&

Quotes:

Heroism

In sign of forgiveness, *shake the hand of your offender only when you can sincerely step above the mountain of his past action.*

Duc du Clos

A promised gauze, *however well intended, can never stop present bleeding.*

Duc du Clos

Despite our natural character, *we often become what is thought and made of us.*

Duc du Clos

When misunderstanding *becomes a sheer weapon for engagement of war, then a simple explanation becomes a clear and evident treaty of peace.*

Duc du Clos

In old centuries, *the word honor was so valued that dishonor was a stain, which could be washed out only with blood.*

Duc du Clos

Ignorance is not at all incurable, when the mind is willing to make proper adjustments.

Duc du Clos

The more you bleed on the training field, the less likely you will on the battlefield.

Duc du Clos

It's always very good to have witnesses; it's even better when your good conscience is yours.

Duc du Clos

We were all born on the hill and have always known that we will end up on the plateau. It is clear that it is our refusal of acceptance which makes our existence unbearable, as we travel down to our scripted destination.

Duc du Clos

You don't train *a soldier at war. You train a soldier for war.*

Duc du Clos

The power *bestowed upon one shall be the tool of prosperous construction, not the weapon of mass destruction.*

Duc du Clos

The taking of a life *is eventually the forfeiture of one's own.*

Duc du Clos

What makes a soldier *a hero is not his own battles nor victories… rather the quest to brave the impossible for others after him… to conquer his ultimate vision.*

Duc du Clos

Being brave *is to stand on your own feet, while knowing in your heart that falling on your face is imminent.*

Duc du Clos

It is extraordinary *what an ordinary mind can do in time of need.*

Duc du Clos

The mind *is a powerful foe. Don't let it become yours.*

Duc du Clos

The element of surprise *is the greatest weapon the mind can ever produce.*

Duc du Clos

***The mere development** of any battle creates an automatic loser, if not two... for at the very least, a loss of safety and security will have been borne, even long after victory.*

Duc du Clos

Our neighbors *are the sudden relatives who have not yet left. With courtesy we should manage to treat them, for our eventual desperate cry for help will only go so far, in time of necessity.*

Duc du Clos

Confrontation is *far to be bravery, for bravery without diplomacy is a dull chisel, which will take a lifetime to carve peace.*

Duc du Clos

Adages, Proverbs & Quotes:

Faith

Education is like faith. *The school and the church may introduce the mind or the spirit, however only its good practice can keep it religiously loyal or studious.*

Duc du Clos

When your ambition *outgrows your planned foundation, your empire can only crumble.*

Duc du Clos

The moment a thought *is born, if with good intention and consideration it is formed, an improvement on the world it already is.*

Duc du Clos

Trust *is like a nest, regardless of its ambitious expected enormity. It is built, a single straw at the time.*

Duc du Clos

As we travel *life's long journey, keep in mind that, rather than a stepping-stone, everyone you meet on the trail is a bridge on the path to your destination.*

Duc du Clos

Live life first *and to its fullest, because when comes time for life to leave you, it will not think twice.*

Duc du Clos

Your faith *is your light; if you turn away from it, it is only good to cast a shadow. Face it, and it will guide you.*

Duc du Clos

Some use religion *as a separate excuse to demonstrate dominant denomination on others of different beliefs.*

Duc du Clos

The natural *is the most intricate and difficult relative aspect to artificially or superficially conceal or alter.*

Duc du Clos

The soul *you may not be is always perceived at first glance. The one you truly are, is always understood in due time, with an intimate look.*

Duc du Clos

Counting is the empty plate of greed. It only makes you aware of how much more you need. That's why one shouldn't even count their blessings, but instead, blindly share them.

Duc du Clos

A glimmer of hope *often outshines the blazing flames of desperation.*

Duc du Clos

God never *teaches lessons one can't learn.*

Duc du Clos

Faith *is like wine in a distant challis, you can't see it, but you have to trust it's in there, even at the hope and volume of one single drop.*

Duc du Clos

Hell is *clearly the path on earth, paved with sharp stones where barefoot, we are forced to travel.*

Duc du Clos

Sharing life's blessings *is a direct deposit into an eternal account with infinite dividends.*

Duc du Clos

A question *only seeks an answer, however, correct or incorrect. It is only trust, which requires the truth.*

Duc du Clos

Harmony *is not just sharing your happiness, but offering happiness in a melodious tone.*

Duc du Clos

The past belongs *to the Devil, the present to you and tomorrow is God's Future Plan.*

Duc du Clos

Secretly appreciate *those who are envious of you, for obviously, within yours is their jealous admiration.*

Duc du Clos

The day *that my faith is challenged is not a test, but rather an invitation for renewals.*

Duc du Clos

Faith *is to believe and trust in what **I** say, rather than what eyes see.*

Duc du Clos

Until you know *exactly how you are created, you should always believe in the sculptor above.*

Duc du Clos

Adages, Proverbs
&
Quotes:

Friendship

Never speak your mind when its foaming bubbles are the result of a heated moment in the pot of possibly regrettable ingredients.

Duc du Clos

If you listen to your friends attentively enough talking about others today, you will clearly hear what will be whispered about you tomorrow.

Duc du Clos

The ill acts you do not do to others won't become a prevention of them unto you, but at least in your heart, you'll know you do not deserve them.

Duc du Clos

Your conscience is the path one takes to the journey of redemption, if it's clear, the fog won't impede your vision.

Duc du Clos

If you care and treat your friends well enough, there's very little you should worry about your enemies.

Duc du Clos

When love becomes an ache, *it should be confined to the heart, where it used to roam so freely and not go to your head.*

Duc du Clos

A loan *to a friend, which is not considered a gift, could ultimately turn out to be worth more than the friendship.*

Duc du Clos

As the world rotates within itself, we should learn to discover better and greater goods within our hearts at every revolution.

Duc du Clos

The butter knife you loan your friend often is returned to you as a steak knife.

Duc du Clos

Playing certain games with friends is sometimes paving a path with enemies' stones.

Duc du Clos

A friend who will not betray you is the friend who does not betray another with you.

Duc du Clos

A mind acting on reluctance is always at best, second on the finish line.

Duc du Clos

Intimidation is the disguise of a vulnerable soul in fear of revelation.

Duc du Clos

Courtesy *is the most powerful weapon of soft persuasion.*

Duc du Clos

Jealousy *among friends is as comforting as a feeding mouse. It will blow sweet breezes as it nibbles on your body to mask the painful sensation as it bites.*

Duc du Clos

*A **true** friendship is won in time, while a pretend one, fades with time.*

Duc du Clos

Favors and transactions *are the two most destructive words in a friendship. While favor is an act owed, transaction is a contractual act, which can be conceived as a toll bridge.*

Duc du Clos

Relationships *are like shoes, if you don't care much about your mate, you'll neither remain a couple… nor a pair.*

Duc du Clos

One has to learn *to have pity on most and consideration for all.*

Duc du Clos

Even a good mind *has bad thoughts. So before a simple misunderstanding grows roots, clarify it, while it's just a seed; as such, you won't have to deal with its buds.*

Duc du Clos

Poetry *is the first side of a triangle, the second being pleasantry and the third, the language of the mind. If you don't speak it, you won't understand it.*

Duc du Clos

Poetry

*The mind is a beautiful art
… when poetically painted*

Duc du Clos

The Silhouette

*As she turned around and away from the incandescent light
her shadow began to give shape to her silhouette
She walked out of the glare
and I was suddenly faced with an image of indescribable beauty*

*I tried to capture her attention, but could not utter a sound
The silence upon me was a force of crippling nature
I felt subdued with emotions of impalpable recovery
She rose before my eyes and to render my mind incapacitated
she glanced... as her gaze pierced right through my soul*

*Afloat I felt, as the white clouds engulfed my being
It seemed beneath me nothing concrete had existence
The imagery of her statuesque silhouette once again reappeared
As if disconnected from her body
her shadow simply walked away*

*I have often wondered and strongly believed
in the omnipotence of love, yet, always thought my heart
under its power, would never succumb*

*With such arrogance...
I may have failed on embracing the dream
an adventure of love, which was meant for me alone
By my misfortune of fate
another's eyes may now be contemplating her beauty*

The Silhouette (cont)

I now realize that...
I often stare without seeing the splendor before me
I may have overlooked images
which my heart could have cherished
Is there a time when love comes twice... a second chance to a heart
a soul which may have missed to yield the calling?

In my distant gaze, I had lost perspective
the only chance to pick the shell harboring the pearl
which is being crushed under the weight of my lamenting shadow
Why was not a sign given?
Will there be another time, when luck, once again smiles my way?

As I sought the pearl which was not mine
I seemed to forego the destiny
one which was bequest upon my existence
In failing to grasp her light, I missed my chance at love
I am now forever lost in her silhouette.

Duc du Clos

The Painted Mind

I remember the morning I took away the virginity
of the pure white, rigid, and silent canvas
Still vivid in my mind, I recall…
My non-challant imagination talks its victim
into picture perfect stillness

My brave, yet reckless fingers guide the brush to a fragile line
engraving a mark of emotion
Gradually, the repetition of strokes renders frailness to my last brush
All the while, as the colors begin to blend
a tumultuous volcanic eruption occurs on the pallet…

Anxiously, I once again gaze at my muse
I watch helplessly with pain, as the figure begins to fritter away
My favorite colors are now the destruction of my inspiration
I start to tremble… and hesitation cripples my shaking hand
In distress, I close my eyes to renew my reverie

Suddenly, it comes upon me…
as I regain inspiration of the lost moment
my fingers, once more, with a soft and gentle grip
hold the brush as it begins to caress the canvas
And surprisingly, again comes the revelation

The Painted Mind (cont)

My fingers passionately succumb to their indulgence
Amazingly, they are wandering from the palette to the rigid canvas
I stare at them, romancing the image so intensely that I am lost
unaware that my feet have become covered in the sand on the shore
as if the existence of the ocean is second to my illusion

All I can feel is the sensation of the brush massaging the canvas
as if it is the stroke of my bare hand on soft and tender skin
Imprisoned, my imagination is at the mercy of this gentle touch
I then gladly embrace the confinement that holds my imagination

The canvas… by losing its pale shade of white
is attaining an indescribable image of beauty
This intricate fantasy gives birth to a painting of pure success
I feel the elation of creating "La Piece de Resistance"

In the end, it became clear it was all a dream…
sadly, an illusion of my zealous vision
As I stood before my easel in tormented agony
I realized in deep sorrow, I had yet to touch the virgin canvas
for I had simply painted in my mind
So… I framed the palette.

An artist never dies as long as his inspiration lives

Duc du Clos

I Matter

In this universe I matter, so I confirm by the space I hold & occupy
Living in general is a breathing puzzle
One of which, I'm an intricate particle, however minute

And as whole, without me, life would have a hole
for I'm in the forefront of where I am
responsible for where it leads and who I am

The imprint I leave behind only reflects the weight of my existence
and no one else's and as such
I am the architect of its indentation and shape

I trust in the power and from whom it is derived
I believe in its purity and faith within myself
And at times, when I don't have a handle on my day and control is
slipping out of my grip, it's because a stronger hand is in charge

And I suddenly let go of the realm to a higher power
If I now feel comforted, light, and overjoyed
it is simply because my shoulders are relieved of my burden

As I watch the renewal of my faith
I know in something greater I believe
and so I'm reminded … in this universe, I matter.

Duc du Clos

The Dix Honest Hombres

Our young country was borne out of the old minds of others
Many hands have lost their shades in the mud of its foundation
Together our protective walls have been strongly erected
The fruits from the heavens have been abundantly imported
It is with such harmonious melody our lives play our symphony
Yet, the standing ovation is only offered to the maestro and his baton
while the diligent musicians silently fade away
All that, a signature of society's diminutive appreciation

We know ignorance is the instrument of the uneducated mind
Its music can only be harmful to the senses
Our ears have misled us, while our eyes too often deceived us
for fear of the unknown is the thickest blindfold we bare
So lets embrace with an open heart, the creation bestowed upon us

Our forefathers envisioned this country with a multi-voice choral
where the tones have their distinguished nuances
So as we confuse "Dix Honest Hombres" for "Dishonest Hombres"
we should understand that together in "French, English & Spanish"
it means: "Ten Honest Men"
and as we further wonder if they are welcome, remember
even Washington "Dit (D) Si (C)"… "Says Yes"!

Duc du Clos

Heroes

On lands far from their own they fall
With patriotism, they heed the call
With words of farewell, without hesitation
Leaving behind loved ones in poignant lamentation
With tears and concerns from family so dear
But duty for country is greater than fear

So young they're deployed, when urgency dictates
Too old they appear as they return to our states
They forgo the pleasures to be home with family
To protect others suffering under tyranny
"Heroes" they're called, as "Angels" is taken
For pride in our country is newly awakened

Our flag raised in victory on deserts and shores
We pray safe return, our faith restores
No medals they need, if they can't see it glow
No flags do we want, unless it's a flow
Vibrantly it waves as it unfurls
For in our hearts it's more precious than pearls

Heroes (cont)

Our own heroes they are, even at enemy's gate
With defiance they march, to an infallible fate
They offer their lives for that of a stranger
And live day to day in constant danger
Mutilated often they return, gone so long
Here back in our arms, where they belong

When the fanfare is gone, life returns to formal
But sadly for them, living is no longer normal
Existence as they knew it is a thing of the past
For in their present mind, anxiety will last
And as the days pass, we forget their great feat
And we turn our heads, while they live in the street

For bravery and valiance, celebrations they deserve
For peace and life, with honor they preserve
Our good fortune here is the price of their fright
And thanks to them we sleep soundly at night
Our wish for all is to come safely home
And so to them, I sincerely dedicate this poem.

Duc du Clos

Dedicated to **Operation Mend**, with special appreciation to Dr. Miller and Ronald A. Katz and all others supporting our troops

The Difference

We each are one and should be proud of such distinction
But difference should be what we make, not what makes us

Each and every day we live is a gift
A chance to make a difference in the life of another
Take the time today to glance
with simple compassion into the eyes of a stranger
someone who's worries affect you not
For the cry you don't hear, still resonates in the heart of another
The tears which are not yours, still bring sorrow to someone else

We should breathe, not just to live, rather to help another to do so
The air one inhales is not of the ration of another
So why, with disdain, do we stare at the passerby?
The sidewalk we don't share can only lead us so far
For it's not the path to our personal heaven

The hand one lends without reservation is always returned richer
If not simply by the warmth of another's, by endless appreciation
Look not to judge, but to advocate the benefit in giving
When our eyes cross the sight of distinctions
think not of the difference between us
but for human sake, the difference we can make…
if aside, we put our differences.

Duc du Clos

Angel

Sweet as you are
there is no way on this earth
that your sweetness would not rise
to bring to this garden an array of flowers
full of your marvelous and gracious scent

Your innocent splendor would leave brushless
the best painter under the sun
as mere colors could not capture your portrait
Emotion would encase the atmosphere of his world

I wonder myself how did I not capitulate
And how did I ever find the exceptional capacity
to put into words and express what seemed indescribable

Your fragrance captivates the imagination
Your beauty is a magnificent gift to this earth
And if one day the words so true
under the fine point of my pen
come to life to describe how really beautiful you are
I'll receive from heaven a trophy
for having formulated an angel.

Duc du Clos

The "Same" Theory

*No two things in the world
or on any planet
can ever be the same
Maybe identical, but never the same*

*For even two drops of water
would have to be captured in two separate capsules
That alone changes all the factors
their density, dimension, and proportions*

*Only we as humans, possess the capacity to remain the same
even as the passing time manages to alter our image
For the heart and soul we have been given
will never change*

*The spirit which constantly surrounds us
often makes us feel light, as it helps us carry our burden
but sometimes heavy when it abandons us
as if the weight of the world is upon our shoulders
All these nuances give the illusion of change in ourselves*

*But, in reality, only situations will change
as the variances of the world will never change mankind
for in theory, we will always be the same.*

Duc du Clos

My Existence

*My existence was kept in a shadow
an old dusty book in the attic of the past
Then you came along and opened my life*

*I now live a beautiful page at a time
I knew not until you, the sweet sensation and touch of another soul
Mine used to soar in search of its destiny
I now know that destiny is not to be sought
rather a paradise to be found in its own time*

*I've been eternally rewarded for my patience of calm expectations
by the gift of you upon me, God has bestowed
And if to you everything I offer
it's because without you
my existence no longer matters*

*You make me see the joy of a heart beating for another
that love can't take flight on a single wing
My soul was a single helpless one, and without yours
could not balance love in the journey to happiness*

*You are now here, and once again, I exist
For your presence is above all, my existence.*

Duc du Clos

Joy and Happiness

*Joy is a temporary and brief excitement
seemingly offered by happiness in a moment of carefree regrets*

*While happiness is a settling contentment of joy…
a lasting feeling at the bottom of the pond that's your heart
a heart which is drenched in the consistent droplets of bliss
It invigorates your days, as the hours pass
It does not foresee potential consequences
for true happiness has none*

*The melodic moment of joy is a song with an ending tune
which often resonates melancholic utterance
It holds your heart responsible for the brief pleasures it once brought
Joy will always be a passing fancy
a glare in the moment of has been*

*Joy is visible, for it sets your eyes aglow
It cares not if, at moments, it's not shared
While happiness is a heavy load when felt and carried alone
for eternally, it seeks out a companion to share its joy*

*Regardless of the quest of your life, let happiness bring you joy
while you enjoy the temporary happiness that joy may bring.*

Duc du Clos

A World Revealed...

... A poet writes the story
about the world to himself
and despite his reluctance
he will be personally known

While some writer's write
about themselves to the world
to enlighten others
and only their world will be revealed.

Duc du Clos

Our Planet

She offers atmosphere and gravity
In return, we quest to triumph over different space
There may be others in the far distant firmament
Which, through our telescopes, we long to conquer
But no matter how high in our shuttles we go
regardless how long in our air balloons we glide
she welcomes us back to earth
in her womb, where we truly belong

In her simple ways she gives us strength and
accepts our indignant treatment
But how long will she last
if with such disregard we treat her crust?

We neglect the one which has given us everything
Her hair we cut, as we deplete her forests
Exposed to the burning sun
through the darkest clouds, her scalp blisters
Have we no heart?

Her branches still protect us, as we build bigger huts
Her frail fingers decorate our quarters, and frame our arts
The crackling of her bones we hear in our fire
When in her dying hour, she still brings us warmth
Have we no consideration?

Our Planet (cont)

Her spine we break to the shape of our rivers
as we navigate streams in search of riches
With rage, we sip the black and thick blood of her veins
as it spills and kills our resources, coating our shores
Have we no conscience?

Her nostrils are clogged from the waving of our polluted hands
In peril is our land, as she struggles to breathe
As we witness the melting of her icebergs
we fail to see those are the maternal tears she sheds

She, like a mother has been to us
And of her loins we are borne
Not enough, do we ever take the time to cherish her
The fervent approach we take in stepping on other planets
would be best used in reducing the deep imprints we are here leaving

Our "planet" has lost its "e", becoming just a "plant"
Why don't we use that "e" for greater "ecology"
And care for the one on which we were born… Our Planet.

Duc du Clos

We should heed global warming as a vital warning …

"I"
Who Am Part Of "IF"

I am the best I could offer to myself
And if by chance I seek to be another
it's because I failed, for a moment, to remember who I am

I will not forgo, if bleak reflections I was born to emanate
for brighter glares illuminating the path of another
If not within myself I can grow and improve
no greater creation was I meant to be
I will be satisfied with the limits of my existence
for no greater one shall I know

I'm fully contented with the person I turned out to be
without once having impeded the existence of another
I've seen the glorious days of those around me yet
neither jealousy nor envy have ever been my source of energy
for they could only hamper my acceptance of their success

I will cherish the differences the Lord has created between us
may they be virtues, riches, or accomplishments
For I am the gift I was given to myself
So I am happy to be me.

Duc du Clos

Love is Like the Sea

Love has the strength of the sea; it destroys as easily as it embraces
It takes you to a longer journey than you planned
It invites you to admire and explore the many wondrous dreams

Love offers its oceans as stages where reality performs
The roles one plays are beyond the wonder of any imagination
The palpitation of the heart is always comforted by the ending
performance, one where love, once again, always takes center stage

Love may be as volatile as the waves
but, it always leaves its tracks on the trail of the sea
The waves never forget the shores they once visited
The carpet of soft sand always retains the path of every wave
because the sand knows love is like the wave; it always comes back

Even when disguised as a tsunami or a simple ripple
love always revisits the shores
And the shore recognizes the distinct touch of every individual wave
as love embraces the shore all around its crevices
leaving behind a fragrance and that salty taste

Yes, love is like the sea, as is your love in my heart
It changes, but never leaves
Yes, our love is like the sea

Duc du Clos

True Friends

*A true friend is never just anyone
but simply one who has evolved with time
as more than just simply anyone
to become special*

*...One who foresees the tears before they are shed
who can anticipate an avalanche of destructive
emotions from the trembling of the lips
before they formulate any sound*

*...One who knows the weight of your tears
because their shoulders have protected your soul
from getting drenched*

*A true friend is the cane and walker of your youth
when your knees give and you succumb
under the pressure of those who are not*

*...One who feels the temperature of your sweat
through personal trials and tribulations
for they are always there to cheer and support*

*...One who does not question
for your friendship is the answer*

True Friends *(cont)*

*A true friend is a mirror in which you see yourself
a true reflection from the water you trust to drink*

*…One to whom you always have so much to say
yet are never in need to
for your mere presence represents enough explanation*

*…One with whom you do more than build memories
for they are always reminding you*

*…One who's not concerned with what they hear
for their heart feels what they know*

*A true friend is one who is always certain
when all others wonder how to be a true friend.*

Duc du Clos

Whole

Too often we seek to be whole
We seem to forget who we are
by losing ourselves into what we are

It is too limited to be whole
Whole has an end
a false impression of completion

As long as we are just a part
we will always belong
belonging to a forever existence
an existence greater than the one we are living

It is the strength of a link
which has survived the passing of time
and is ready to outlive the future

I'm happy to now recognize that I am a part
an intricate part in a life that has a past
seen the plans and helped the making of now

Whole (cont)

I have certainty of being an inextricable part of what's to come
Tomorrow will not deny the breaths I inhale today
Another part will connect to exhale as I take my last breath

However hard we may try
one can never write his own history
just the story of one's life
Any day may become the last days of our lives

Yet we should take solace in knowing that
it is not the last day of life
a life of which we will always be a part

As long as a part of us lives in others
we will then never die
For we may be apart
yet we will always be a part of forever.

Duc du Clos

The Art of Science

Science is an Art
While there can't exist Art without Science
Science itself does, as it is a museum, with its own Art
Life without Art would be bleak, mute and motionless
as Art awakens our senses

Art is a medium of expression
with a momentary application of an artistic mind
May the art be permanent or passing
it will always be self-expressed
which is why art is susceptible to performance and reception
when science is infallible

Science is a fact, and as such, can't ever be wrong
The factual events may be misconstrued, misplaced
miscalculated, misjudged or misrepresented
even changed from right to wrong or visa-versa
The fact will remain that they are within themselves, facts

Science… its combination, formula, conclusion or discovery
however minute, may differ from one to another
As a result, the scientist may be wrong
but Science never is

The Art of Science (cont)

*Although Art and Science walk hand in hand
this notion of relation is clearly understood
under the scientific artifact in the gallery of life
that it will always be that Art needs Science
But Science is itself an Art, and does not need Art
which is the Art of Science.*

Duc du Clos

A good friend

*... is not necessarily someone who is there for you all the time
but one who gives you personal room to grow*

*... is not someone who simply takes refuge under your foliage
but comes around in seasons when the yellow and
brown leaves of your days need to be picked up*

*...is not someone who uproots and branches out to greener forests
but sticks around when branches of your years
need to be pruned and trimmed*

*... is not someone who neglects to share lessons learned
but instead uses them as a compass to guide your path*

*... is not someone who calls to boost their sense of self
but one who borrows time to lend an ear*

*... is not someone who feels the need to compete, control
nor influence, but above and beyond it all*

... is simply a good friend.

Duc du Clos

The Romantic

We carry a sacred secret as if it was forbidden
We collapse and submerge under the thought of being discovered
Because of its uncommon value, we hide a natural virtue
which is offered to very few

Just as any magnificent gift, romance is to be shared
We live in a reverie, and spend our youth
dreaming of expressing the language of the heart
for it is the only one we need to communicate our love

We live in a world of malefic dominance
And there exists those who only travel on the path of broken hearts
For they have never known the profound pleasure of love

We are forced to embrace clandestinely
so not to expose the object of their malfeasance
A love as pure as ours will one day see the light of day and
without a care, we will openly display the sentiments of our hearts

Love often conquers the heart of even those who have lost theirs
It is the only emotion, which will always live with the notion
that it can triumph over all the misconceptions of a failed destiny
For as long as there is love, we all have the chance to be romantic.

Duc du Clos

A Shade Apart

I was fortunate enough to grow up in a time and place where the beautiful rainbow we have come to admire was, for me, at the peak of its birth. For the clouds and the snow, virginally vibrant, moved us with their beauty. The yellow reflection of the sun on the horizon was of immense splendor. The days were clear and neutral to our senses.

As for us, we were then simply different, human beings just a shade apart, a slight shadow with a different shape in a form of personal distinction. Minority was exactly the minimal number in a mathematical expression, and majority, well… the other end of the spectrum. We have always known that there is power in numbers, and number was all that it was.

Now, for some reason, when we hear the word minority we simply and clearly deduct, not a numerical cadence, but rather, a classification of complexion. It even dwindles down to the point where the awards we display on walls or shelves, though bearing our names, become more important to others than to us. It is evident that success has its own complexion.

As a child, shame and pride were the main components of respect. One could not have one without the other. Nowadays, respect seems to be proudly standing exempt of shame.

A Shade Apart (cont)

We have to value who and what surround us, by keeping in mind that as long as someone else inhales what you exhale, you then become part of a society. As such, consideration should become the governing body. The moment one stops taking into equation the affect of one's behavior on others, only then should one become a minority. We should all try to pass on to our children, the importance of walking this earth hand in hand.

Complexion matters a lot to some; as to them, it's the most secure, yet unfair way to recognize the enemy. But before the next judgment is formed, consider this… Could this living be a test or an illusion? What if you wake up in the complexion of your enemy, would it be the nightmare of your life?

Could you turn out to be someone else and still accept yourself in a different complexion? Would you be happy living this possible dream, or are you scared to wake up and live the real life?

Before you wake up and make a choice, remember, we are all a multitude of the same colors, and simply a shade apart.

Duc du Clos

The Demon Within

Born from the fruit of innocence, we finally see the sun's first ray
We cherish its sight at any offered occasion
It lights up our day when the moon kisses other horizons
It is the natural energy we seek to restore our strengths
How could we ever have known its beauty was menacing?

Grown from the tree of our ancestors
proudly we branch out and away from our roots
only to discover that the hereditary bark we've come to know
may eventually become our source of vulnerability
We live a life unaware of its inner strengths and weaknesses
Yet, they are tested in the most unexpected and enduring times
Victorious for some and so sadly unfortunate for many
The strength of the oak shall the weak twig find in turbulent winds
Too many souls have been drowned in the name of departed ones

One day the miracle which is owed, will come to be, and
slowly and happily, we'll develop into the creature we're meant to be
As time goes by, we'll learn to live and love to the extent of our hearts
The maladies we have suffered will be mysteries no more
For a cure shall be found to end the miseries of all
Obstacles to surely overcome will they be and not a sign of final rites
For eternally, the body is pure and the day is near
With the demons within, we live no more.

To the Survivors, Spirits and Souls reading upon our shoulders.

Duc du Clos

The Prose and Cons of A Poem

A poem has its pros and cons
as it does its prose and cons
A pro will help you with a verse
While a con will steal your universe

An artist, he believes he is, with all his tricks
When all his poems are nothing but limericks
A poem may leave you melancholic
As another will allow you freedom to be melodramatic

One may have a good form of structure
Another will bend you out of shape into bad posture
One could play tunes to your heart as a ballad
Making you feel very content or even make you sad

A poem will try to find rhythm and rhyme
But many will be just a waste of time
And some will continue to no end as an epic
While others will meet an end, that's oh, so very tragic

Most poems move you with their many tenses
As you read through, they affect all your senses
That's why I believe that everyone knows
There's no better way to say it, than in a simple prose.

Duc du Clos

The Punctuation Points
to ponder ...

is a "clamation" which use to be ...	! **Ex clamation**
is always in critical condition...	, **comma**
is half way there ...	; **semi-colon**
gets help at home ...	( ) **parent heses**
is strict and direct ...	. **period**
is the fastest ...	- **dash / hyphen**
is the most famous of them all...	* **star**
is champion of them all ...	' **apos-trophy**
always keeps you on your toes...	... **3 point suspension**
holds you safely together...	[ ] **brackets**
is in the army	<< >>
is a point of attainment	" " **quota-tion**

Duc du Clos

My Child

*You have made our lives so complete
envied by those who have witnessed you grow
The ease at which you always set our minds
is befitting of an earth-walking angel*

*As you depart for a farther destination
take with you the assurance of our pure love
Know you will sadly leave our nest with a void
no creature, twig, nor the mighty oak can fulfill*

*No effort is ample to appease your absence
for it will fail to alleviate our sadness
May you find comfort in every step on your trail
May the stone beneath your feet secure your soul*

*May the winds of change, affect not your character
Yet, may they help you soar as you unfold your wings
May your thirst for knowledge guide you to the fountain of sweetest
and freshest water and may that desire be satisfied; yet unquenched*

*As you embark in this cultural and academic journey
bring and share with this new world the joy, happiness, and love you
have blessed upon us, for it is the only comfort consoling our hearts
knowing, that this world is in for a much needed change.*

Duc du Clos

Me

Selfish was I, for life itself was about me
The "me" I painted with borrowed brushes
with impeccable strokes, on the canvas that's my existence
I patiently penciled in the perfect picture
of the person I needed to be

And in time, as the colors dried, I could clearly see
the self-portrait of a soul with a different character
The traits were not at all those of my youthful imagination
where the muse was captured with vivid composition
posing at an angle, which captivated the light of day

It was the performance of a lifetime
the image of the person I could have been
Now life as I value it, belongs to those around me
whom I love so dearly, who are the frame, in which
even I, as any imperfect picture, belong

No regrets should I have, no repentance shall I seek
for no wrong in my heart I have done
Yet, once in a while, if in a mirror I stare
it is simple to reassure myself, that the reflection is not of me
but that of the people who now make my life worthwhile

Me (cont)

*And that the ME I knew for so long was just a mere
misunderstanding of a W, which was upside down
and before a lonely E, as was my life before
The people who love me make me realize that life is not at all about
the ME, but the WE, who love one another.*

Dedicated to the souls who have conquered and changed mine.

Duc du Clos

MY PRAYER

Dear Lord
Creator of all
Thank you O Lord for this instant
Each breath I take is another sign of your existence
Give me the capacity to accept my neighbors as brothers
Remove from my heart any flow of jealousy
so my veins may be pure
Cleanse my spirit of my burdens
before another night envelops my soul

Bestow upon me the strength to forgive
even against my unwillingness to do so
Point to my heart the beauty, which my eyes failed to see
Show me the best in everyone, though such, they may not display
Help me renew myself and wash away my sins
Forsake me not in my time of need, for I only seek your pardon

Allow me another day so I can have one more chance to pray
As I look up to you, please let not the sun disturb my sight
for I only seek to find your light in the Heavens
Forgive me for the pain I may not be aware
of having brought unto my brothers
If by your judgment I am found at fault
on me cast your veil of guilt

MY PRAYER (cont)

*I repent for any thought of malfeasance
which may have crossed my mind
Show me the way to salvation
though no wrong I may have done
I know, the path to redemption is traveled only by sinners
but on it, I will gladly walk
if it will lead to your door*

*Who was I to ever believe that I needed but myself
in a world so vast where love's so rare
and so little of it is ever found
Let my way be paved, not with temptations
but a clear sign of redemption
How will I know when you're near?
Not knowing for sure, every face I now meet, I'll cherish
Please guide me lord, for I pray to you*

*I know the pain you have endured for us
the sufferance you have been subjected to
I should have learned from the lessons you have taught
But Lord forgive me, for I am your child
And please teach me once more
So I may love, accept and be whole again.*

Duc du Clos

You, Once Again

After you've gone, I tried so many other temptations
But my heart, faithful to you, is holding on to past emotions
I tried to visit places where we used to go
There, in the midst of the crowd your voice still has it's own echo

I even saw friends we used to know
But on everyone's face, yours haunts me so
And now I'd like to give up everything I own
But nothing would ever change the fact that you're gone

Now I cry with all my heart at the sound of our song
And it's been hurting for it still lingers on the tip of my tongue
Others tried to comfort and cheer my soul
But on my heart, the passing time is taking its toll

I can't go on wanting what may never return to be
When I know in my heart, you should be more than a memory
Please take the time to inventory the past of your heart
And you'll find that we should have never come to part

You, Once Again (cont)

It's you once again, no matter where I travel
That face which made me once happy and marvel
Not before my eyes, but still engraved deep inside of me
Is the picture of you, the way we used to be

You often take me to places so real in my dreams
So vivid in my sleep to me reality always it seems
Don't believe in paradise, couldn't care less about heaven
I'd trade them both for one night with you once again.

Duc du Clos

The Dove Of Rome

Born out of the ruins of ancient time
The constant turbulence of falling rocks
kept her alert as to stay alive
She never knew the comfort of a nest
where on soft hay she could rest her lovely head

Among the debris of an abandoned medieval temple
there, between some rocks, she found refuge
protected from the many forces of nature greater than hers

She has never known the freedom of the flight of the candor
For in the sky above, has always been her greatest fear
The coat of dust she wears
is reminiscent of her ancestors' old plumage
Yet, she would never know
for she's never seen another of common feather
but in the reflection of waters

Like the ruins, she too, was left broken and to be forgotten
She only finds solace when the cold wind blows
and the breeze whispers soft melodies
through the chaos and slumbers of broken pillars
columns, which once supported the magnificent edifices of kings
She felt that, albeit her melancholic existence
her life was created with a purpose

The Dove Of Rome (cont)

Just like love, she too belongs to a heart
And soon enough she'll conquer the open sky
For when a dove flies
destiny writes a message of love in the air
From the palm of a lucky recipient
Love will find a heart
For the lonely dove of Rome
holds the most Rome antique love of all.

Duc du Clos

Time

*As we take in our initial breath
our eyes see, for the first time
the beautiful rays of light
And from that moment on
we lose any notion of time*

*In a rush to make up for time lost
which we never possessed in the first place
we stumble within ourselves
as if we were late to our ever moving destination
We hurry the hours
as we skip the days*

*Suddenly, the clock of our lives
misses a familiar tic
and we finally realize how lonely a tock can be
We try in the midst of it all
to hastily accomplish the impossible*

*Regardless of all we do to grasp it
we need to remember that
time runs on its own schedule
Time only requests that
we pay just a little attention and accord to its passing*

Time (cont)

Despite its neglect
time is our best and longest gift
Yet, we watch it go by with so very little care

Time only slips through our fingers
if we don't hand it out
and share it with those we love
Too often we wait simply to realize
how precious it really is

So don't wait to cherish it
Most of all, spend it with loved ones
Embrace the moment a day ago
For only now is time
After now, it may very well never be time again.

In memory of... **Count François Marie Louis de Maigret**

Duc du Clos

Night

*At night, I can't wait to go to bed, because I realize
to my wondrous surprise, every morning, day by day
how much more I grow to love you
And to think after all of these years of loving you
I, by now, should be used to wanting you so desperately*

*How can a soul be so thirsty for comfort?
Every time you look at me, inside of myself I feel lost
I go lightheaded with a heart drowning in love
Even as I dream of you portraying an angel
please wake me up for the real you I long for*

*Help me spend another day in the paradise of your arms
Invite my heart to keep yours company
What is a day if not with you it is spent?
I will always cherish our days, however long
But give me the night, for it always adds to our love.*

Duc du Clos

The Mind Is Like A Shelf

The mind is like a shelf
Like a child's, it is empty and strong
and very apt to receive whatever the future holds
which is why a child can easily learn a new language

As adult's, with volumes of information, the shelf becomes full
Under such weight of maturity, its foundation weakens
as its center caves under the stress of remembrance
It is not so much we forget, rather we fail to grasp the inevitable
as our shelves surrender under the compilation of the past

Our mind often attempts to evade the accumulation of life's gifts
We take for granted the necessity to make room for new thoughts
thoughts we believe would simply fade away in our memory bin

On the shelf, we often reach out to relive a moment of the past
But our brittle present, unaware of the weight of the memory
succumbs under the dust of days gone by

Until we recognize that the shelf is the library of our lives
we will never cherish it to the value of the mind
for the mind is like the shelf.

Duc du Clos

Dad

Dear Dad,

    This poem was to be my first, and in my heart, before the touch of a pen, it began so very long ago. However, each time I attempt to express myself, I am consumed with such profound sadness that I cannot continue. I find myself losing the capacity to put into words, the magnificence of you. It seems my gift of words has, when I needed it most, failed me... Thus, I'm left with this space, which reflects the void in my heart, an eternal hole in which I am still falling ...

... Please forgive me dad, for I cannot pull the drowning words out of the ocean of my endless tears. Gratefully, like any love, it needs not to be expressed, to be felt. Fortunately, as the days pass, I feel your love through everyone else around me, with whom it is shared. It is in remembering the compassion and affection of you I always find comfort.

    Please stretch your wings to the span of protecting my family. Thank you for still looking over me. I miss you so much!

                            Your Blessed son,
                            Duc

Thank-You!

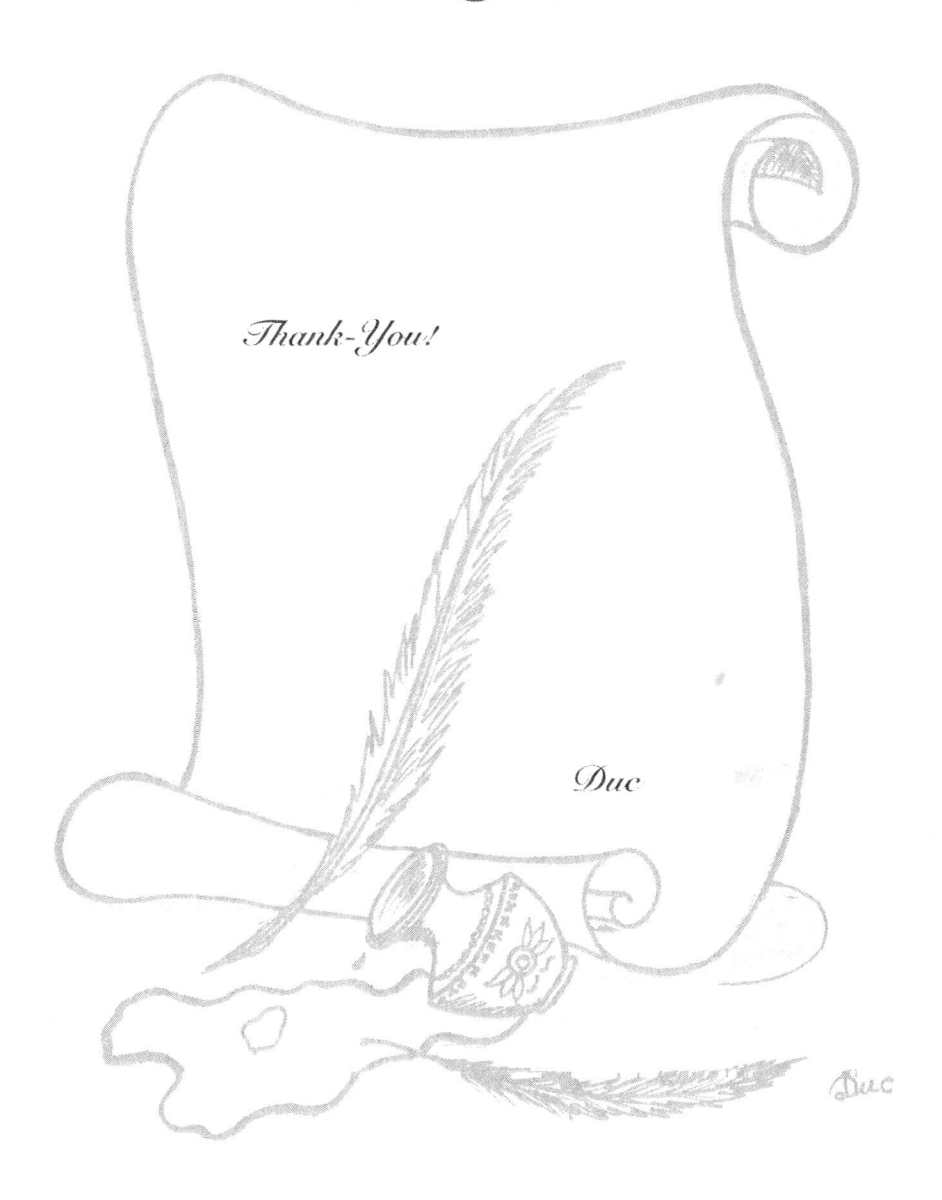

Duc

Old Echoes of a New Voice

Original Works Of

Duc du Clos

*Fame is somewhat like the Liberty Bell.
It is not always what it is cracked up to be,
for it is louder to the sight than to the sound*